Fiona Mapp

D1407154

ESSENTIALS

Year 9
KS3 Mathematics
Coursebook

How to Use this Coursebook

A Note to the Teacher

This coursebook includes coverage of the Level 1 Functional Skills for Maths appropriate to Year 9. Guidance and practice material relating to these skills is integrated into the main content of the book to reflect the structure of the new Programme of Study.

Each coursebook comprises...
- clear, concise content appropriate to that year
- questions and tasks to reinforce students' learning and help improve their confidence.

Where appropriate, the coursebooks relate mathematical concepts to real-life situations, to illustrate the importance of maths beyond the classroom.

This Year 9 coursebook is split into 19 topics. Each topic has the following features:
- **Content** that students need to learn.

- **Key words** picked out in colour in the text and listed at the end of the section.
- A **Quick Test** to assess students' understanding through a combination of theory-based questions, multiple choice questions and true/false questions.
- **Skills Practice** questions to provide students with the opportunity to practise what they have learned.

Selected topics have an **extension activity** to further reinforce students' understanding. These take the form of a practical activity or investigation.

Also included in the centre of the book is a pull-out answer booklet. It contains the answers to all of the questions in this coursebook.

Each coursebook is supported by a workbook to provide further practice and help consolidate learning.

A Note to the Student

We're sure you'll enjoy using this coursebook, but follow these helpful hints to make the most of it:
- Try to write answers that require reasoning or explanation in good English, using correct punctuation and good sentence construction. Read what you have written to make sure it makes sense.
- Think carefully when drawing graphs. Always make sure that you have labelled your axes, given your graph a title and plotted points accurately.
- Try to learn what all the key words mean.

- Where questions require you to make calculations, remember to show your workings. In tests, you might get marks for a correct method even if you arrive at the wrong answer.
- The tick boxes on the Contents page let you track your progress: simply put a tick in the box next to each topic when you're confident that you know it.

You might need a calculator to answer questions that carry this symbol. All other questions should be attempted without using a calculator and you should show your workings.

Contents

Numbers

Rounding Numbers

Numbers are rounded frequently as this makes them easier to work with. They can be rounded to the nearest 10, 100, 1000, etc. Decimals can be rounded to a particular number of decimal places (d.p.).

17.639 = 17.64 (2 d.p.)

1.5983 = 1.598 (3 d.p.)

263.55 = 263.6 (1 d.p.)

Significant Figures

To find the 1st **significant figure** (s.f. or sig. fig.) look for the the first digit which is not zero. The 2nd, 3rd, 4th... significant figures may or may not be zero.

After rounding the last digit you must fill in the end zeros. For example, 525 = 530 to 2 s.f.

Examples

Number	to 3 s.f.	to 2 s.f.	to 1 s.f.
2.715	2.72	2.7	3
5273	5270	5300	5000
0.06883	0.0688	0.069	0.07

Estimating and Approximating

Estimating can be used to check your answers. For example, it's useful when decorating to estimate the number of tins of paint needed.

When estimating...
- round the numbers to easy numbers, 1 or 2 s.f.
- use 0.1, 0.01, etc. when multiplying or dividing, not zero
- use the symbol ≈ as this means 'approximately equal to'
- small numbers can be approximated to zero when adding or subtracting.

Examples

$9.7 \times 4.1 \approx 10 \times 4 = 40$

$0.073 \times 51 \approx 0.1 \times 50 = 5$

$\frac{795 + 106}{2.7 \times 3.1} \approx \frac{800 + 100}{3 \times 3} = \frac{900}{9} = 100$

$299.9 + 0.001 \approx 300 + 0 = 300$

Upper and Lower Bounds

When a number has been rounded to a given number of significant figures you might need to know the largest and smallest values the number may have been. These are called the **upper** and **lower bounds** of the number.

Examples

1 62 000 (2 s.f.) people watched Liverpool's football game this weekend. What are the lower and upper bounds of the numbers of supporters?

People or items can only take a whole number value. You can't have a fraction of a person.

the smallest number that rounds up to 62 000

the largest number that rounds down 62 499 ← to 62 000

61 500   62 000   62 500

The lower bound = 61 500 supporters
The upper bound = 62 499 supporters

2 A piece of string is 6.3cm correct to the nearest centimetre. Write down the lower and upper bounds of the piece of string.

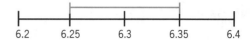

6.2   6.25   6.3   6.35   6.4

The lower bound = 6.25cm
The upper bound = 6.35cm

The piece of string can be any length up to 6.35cm.

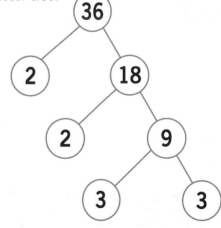

Laws of Indices

5^7 means $5 \times 5 \times 5 \times 5 \times 5 \times 5 \times 5$.

5 is the **base** and 7 is the **power** of the **index**.

When multiplying the powers of the same numbers you add the indices.

Example
$5^4 \times 5^3 = (5 \times 5 \times 5 \times 5) \times (5 \times 5 \times 5)$
$= 5^{4+3}$
$= 5^7$

When dividing powers of the same number you subtract the indices.

Example
$5^6 \div 5^4 = \dfrac{\cancel{5} \times \cancel{5} \times \cancel{5} \times \cancel{5} \times 5 \times 5}{\cancel{5} \times \cancel{5} \times \cancel{5} \times \cancel{5}}$
$= 5^{6-4}$
$= 5^2$

> You need to know how to use the power key on your calculator.

Any number (other than zero) raised to the power of zero equals 1.

Example
$5^0 = 1$
$6^0 = 1$
$100^0 = 1$

Prime Factors

Some numbers can be written as the **product** of their **prime factors**.

Example
The prime factors of 36 can be shown on a prime factor tree.

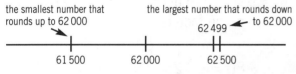

```
        36
       /  \
      2    18
          /  \
         2    9
             /  \
            3    3
```

- Divide 36 by its first prime factor, 2.
- Divide 18 by its first prime factor, 2.
- Keep on until the final number is prime.

As a product of its prime factors, 36 may be written as:

$36 = 2 \times 2 \times 3 \times 3$
$= 2^2 \times 3^2$

Numbers

Highest Common Factor

You need to know the highest common factor (**HCF**) when you're factorising.

Example

Find the HCF of 80 and 56.

1. Write the numbers as a product of their prime factors.

   $80 = 2 \times 2 \times 2 \times 2 \times 5$
   $56 = 2 \times 2 \times 2 \qquad \times 7$

2. Circle the common factors.

   These give the HCF as $2 \times 2 \times 2 = 8$.

   The HCF of 80 and 56 is 8.

Lowest Common Multiple

You need to know the lowest common multiple (**LCM**) when you're adding and subtracting fractions.

Example

Find the LCM of 80 and 56.

1. Write the numbers as a product of their prime factors.

   $80 = 2 \times 2 \times 2 \times 2 \times 5$
   $56 = 2 \times 2 \times 2 \qquad \times 7$

   Line the columns up carefully. Take one number from each column.

2. The LCM of 80 and 56 is:
   $2 \times 2 \times 2 \times 2 \times 5 \times 7 = 560$

Quick Test

1. Work out an estimate to $\dfrac{29.2 \times 41.6}{6.1}$

2. Round the following to 2 s.f.
   - **a)** 2735
   - **b)** 9.647
   - **c)** 2.075

3. The LCM of 12 and 20 is 60. True or false?

4. $5° = 5$. True or false?

KEY WORDS

Make sure you understand these words before moving on!

- Significant figure
- Estimation
- Upper bound
- Lower bound
- Base
- Power
- Index
- Product
- Prime factor
- HCF
- LCM

Skills Practice

1 True or false?
- **a)** 492 = 490 to 2 s.f.
- **b)** 1057 = 106 to 3 s.f.
- **c)** 4476 = 5000 to 1 s.f.
- **d)** 279 = 300 to 1 s.f.
- **e)** 1955 = 2000 to 2 s.f.
- **f)** 476 = 48 to 2 s.f.
- **g)** 10071 = 10070 to 5 s.f.
- **h)** 605 = 610 to 2 s.f.

2 By rounding each number to 1 s.f. find an approximate answer to…
- **a)** 921×407
- **b)** 36×19
- **c)** 204×1599
- **d)** $\dfrac{8576 - 10.2}{10.1}$

3 Simplify…
- **a)** $4^5 \times 4^2$
- **b)** $3^6 \times 3^2$
- **c)** $4^2 \times 4^5$
- **d)** $6^3 \times 6^2$
- **e)** $10^7 \div 10^3$
- **f)** $6^9 \div 6^2$
- **g)** $7^4 \div 7^1$
- **h)** $8^6 \div 8^3$

4 Work out the index missing from each box.
- **a)** $2^4 \times 2^\square = 2^{10}$
- **b)** $12^\square \div 12^2 = 12^{20}$
- **c)** $3^\square \div 3^5 = 3^3$
- **d)** $6^\square \times 6^2 = 6^7$

5 Find the prime factors of…
- **a)** 25
- **b)** 42
- **c)** 72

6 Find the HCF and LCF of…
- **a)** 20 and 45
- **b)** 16 and 28
- **c)** 32 and 60

7 For each of these statements, write the upper and lower bound.
- **a)** There are 620 people in a hall, to 2 s.f.
- **b)** There are 5600 supporters at a second division football club, to 2 s.f.
- **c)** The population of Cardiff is 157 000, to 3 s.f.
- **d)** The height of a tree is 2.7 metres, to 1 d.p.
- **e)** There are 3550 ants in an ant colony, to 3 s.f.

Fractions, Decimals & Ratio

Adding and Subtracting Fractions

You should already know that only fractions with the same denominators can be added or subtracted.

Examples

1 $\dfrac{2}{7} + \dfrac{7}{10}$

Change the fractions to their equivalents with a denominator of 70 and rewrite the sum.

$$\dfrac{20}{70} + \dfrac{49}{70} = \dfrac{69}{70}$$

2 $3\frac{1}{4} - 2\frac{5}{12}$

Rewrite as an improper fraction.

$$\dfrac{13}{4} - \dfrac{29}{12}$$

$$= \dfrac{39}{12} - \dfrac{29}{12}$$

$$= \dfrac{10}{12} = \dfrac{5}{6}$$

Multiplying and Dividing Fractions

When you're asked to multiply and divide fractions, you should remember to write whole or mixed numbers as improper fractions.

Example

Multiply...

$$1\frac{2}{3} \times 2\frac{4}{5}$$

$$= \dfrac{\overset{1}{5}}{3} \times \dfrac{14}{\underset{1}{5}}$$

 Multiply the numerators together

Multiply the denominators together

Cancel any fractions first. Give the answer as a mixed number.

$$= \dfrac{14}{3} = 4\frac{2}{3}$$

For division, take the reciprocal of the second fraction (i.e. turn it upside down) and multiply the fractions together.

Example

$$4\frac{2}{3} \div \dfrac{2}{9}$$

$$= \dfrac{14}{3} \div \dfrac{2}{9}$$

$$= \dfrac{14}{\underset{1}{3}} \times \dfrac{\overset{3}{9}}{2}$$

$$= \dfrac{14}{3} = 21$$

The Fraction Key on a Calculator

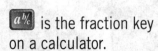 is the fraction key on a calculator.

$2\frac{1}{3}$ is keyed in as

Decimals

A **terminating decimal** is a decimal that ends.

Example

$$0.637 = \dfrac{6}{10} + \dfrac{3}{100} + \dfrac{7}{1000} = \dfrac{637}{1000}$$

A **recurring decimal** is a decimal where one or more figures repeat.

Example

0.6666... is written as $0.\dot{6}$

0.373737... is written as $0.\dot{3}\dot{7}$

Multiplying and Dividing Numbers Between 0 and 1

When multiplying numbers between 0 and 1, the result is smaller than the starting value.

Examples
$72 \times 0.1 = 7.2$
$72 \times 0.01 = 0.72$
$72 \times 0.001 = 0.072$

When dividing numbers between 0 and 1, the result is bigger than the starting value.

Examples
$63 \div 0.1 = 630$ Since $63 \div 0.1 = 63 \div \frac{1}{10} = 63 \times 10$
$63 \div 0.01 = 6300$ or $\frac{63}{0.01} = \frac{6300}{1} = 6300$
$63 \div 0.001 = 63\,000$

Ordering Decimals

Remember when ordering decimals to use the same number of digits after the decimal point, and then compare the whole numbers, followed by the digits in the correct order.

Example
Arrange these numbers in order of size, smallest first.
52.06, 51.72, 50.769, 51.715, 51.296, 52.073, 52.172

Rewrite them...
52.060, 51.720, 50.769, 51.715, 51.296, 52.073, 52.172

> The 1 tenth is worth less than the 2 tenths

Then order them...
50.769, 51.296, 51.714, 51.720, 52.060, 52.073, 52.172

Powers of 10

The powers of 10 are...
$10^0 = 1$
$10^1 = 10$
$10^2 = 100$
$10^3 = 1000$, etc.

When the power of 10 is smaller than zero, we use a negative power...
$10^{-1} = 0.1$
$10^{-2} = 0.01$
$10^{-3} = 0.001$
$10^{-4} = 0.0001$

Which means...
$\frac{1}{10} = 0.1 = 10^{-1} = 10\%$

Ratio

When you see this symbol : you are dealing with ratio.

To simplify ratios divide both parts of the ratio by their highest common factor.

    30 : 50   Divide both parts by 10
=   3 : 5

Fractions, Decimals & Ratio

Calculations Involving Ratio

You'll need to be able to recognise questions in which ratio is needed as you might not be told to use it.

Examples

1 At a bank Sukhvinder changes £400 into 2560 Dirhams. How many Dirhams would Sukhvinder get for changing £270?

£400 = 2560 Dirhams

£1 = $\frac{2560}{400}$ = 6.4

£270 = 270 × 64
      = 1728 Dirhams

2 The same type of washing powder is sold in three different sized packs (see alongside). Which pack represents the best value for money?

Change kilograms into grams.

780g = £1.92	1g costs	192 ÷ 780 = 0.246
2.4kg = £4.32	1g costs	432 ÷ 2400 = 0.18
3kg = £6.73	1g costs	673 ÷ 3000 = 0.224

Since the 2.4kg pack costs less per gram it is the best value for money.

Quick Test

1 The ratio 6 : 18 fully simplified is 1 : 3. True or false?

2 £27 000 is divided in the ratio 4 : 5. How much is the smaller share?

3 657 × 0.02 = 13.14. True or False?

4 Arrange these decimals in order of size... 6.37, 6.49, 6.04, 6.371, 6.27

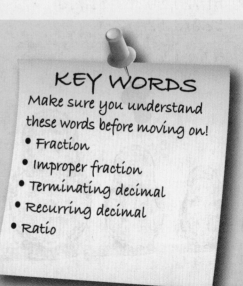

KEY WORDS
Make sure you understand these words before moving on!
• Fraction
• Improper fraction
• Terminating decimal
• Recurring decimal
• Ratio

Skills Practice

1 Work out...

  a) $\frac{2}{7} + \frac{6}{11}$ **c)** $2\frac{1}{5} + 3\frac{2}{3}$

  b) $\frac{4}{5} - \frac{1}{3}$ **d)** $6\frac{1}{9} - 4\frac{1}{3}$

2 Work out...

  a) $\frac{2}{5} \times \frac{3}{7}$ **c)** $4\frac{1}{5} \times \frac{7}{8}$

  b) $2\frac{1}{2} \times 3\frac{1}{3}$ **d)** $\frac{7}{15} \times 2\frac{1}{3}$

3 Work out...

  a) $\frac{4}{7} \div \frac{1}{3}$ **c)** $2\frac{1}{3} \div 4\frac{1}{7}$

  b) $\frac{2}{3} \div \frac{1}{4}$ **d)** $3\frac{1}{8} \div 2\frac{1}{3}$

4 Round these numbers to 2 decimal places.

  a) 6.479   **c)** 25.416

  b) 17.235   **d)** 9.384

5 Estimate, by rounding the numbers to 1 significant figure, the answer to: $\dfrac{61.5 \times 2.9}{(3.1)^2}$

6 The following distances were thrown in a javelin competition. Arrange the distances in order of size, smallest first.

7.37m, 12.63m, 12.06m, 12.39m, 12.41m, 12.04m

7 If $62 \times 0.02 = 1.24$, what is the answer to 6.2×0.002?

8 7 water bottles cost £10.64. How much do 11 water bottles cost?

9 There are 320 daffodils and iris plants in a garden in the ratio 5 : 3. How many daffodils are there?

Percentages

Percentages

We see percentages all the time in everyday life. A percentage is a fraction with a denominator of 100.

Increasing and Decreasing by a Percentage

You can choose to use either of the following methods to solve increases and decreases by a percentage.

Example
In a sale a bed is reduced by 20%. Find the sale price if the bed originally cost £499.

Method 1
20% of £499

$\frac{20}{100} \times 499 = 99.80$

£499 − £99.80 = £399.20

(For a non-calculator method, work out 10% by dividing by 10 then multiply by 2 to find 20%.)

Method 2
This time we use a multiplier method.

A 20% decrease is a multiplier of 100 − 20 = 80% = 0.8

£499 × 0.8 = £399.20

If you had a 20% increase this would have been added to 100.
100 + 20 = 120% = 1.2
The multiplier would be 1.2

One Quantity as a Percentage of Another

There are many situations where you may need to find a quantity as a percentage of another quantity.

Example

Charlotte got 64 out of 82 in a Science test. What percentage did Charlotte get (to the nearest percentage)?

1 Check that the units are the same and then write as a fraction.

$$\frac{64}{82}$$

2 Then multiply by 100

$$\frac{64}{82} \times 100 = 78\%$$

Profit and Loss

Profit and loss calculations are used in everyday life.

Percentage **profit** (or **loss**)

$$= \frac{\text{Profit (or loss)}}{\text{Original}} \times 100$$

Examples

1 Jonathan bought a motorbike for £8500. Four years later he sold it for £5150. Work out his percentage loss.

cost price – selling price = 8500 – 5150
= £3350

percentage loss $\frac{3350}{8500} \times 100 = 39.4\%$
(1 d.p.)

2 Rupinder bought a time-share for £89 000. Six years later she sold it for £137 000. Work our her percentage profit.

profit = 137 000 – 89 000
= £48 000

percentage profit $\frac{48\,000}{89\,000} \times 100 = 53.9\%$
(1 d.p.)

Effect of the Recession

When there's a 'credit crunch' money is more difficult to borrow on mortgages. After 10 years of growth in the housing market, in 2007 / 2008 the price of properties started to fall. Negative equity is when the value of a property is less than the mortgage owed on it.

The UK housing market experienced one of the largest 'unexplained' increases in property prices over the past decade. Prices were 20-30% higher in 2008 than could be justified by 'fundamentals' such as rising population or higher incomes. Due to the recession, housing markets turned down across western Europe and houses subsequently lost much of their increased value.

Percentages

Repeated Percentage Change

Use multipliers to find the increase or decrease of a quantity over a period of time.

Example

A block of shares was bought for £156 000 in 2006. Each year the value of the shares fell by 8%. Work out the value of the shares after three years.

Decrease of 8% is a multiplier of...

$(100 - 8) = 92\% = 0.92$

Value of shares = 156 000 × 0.92 × 0.92 × 0.92

year 1 year 2 year 3

= £121 457.33

Alternatively write the equation as

$156\,000 \times 0.92^3 = £121\,475.33$

Simple Interest

Simple interest is the interest that is sometimes paid on money in banks and building societies. The interest is paid each year (per annum or p.a.) and is the same amount each year.

Example

Asif has £1500 in his savings account. Simple interest is paid at 4.5% p.a. How much does Asif have in his account at the end of the year?

Increasing by 4.5% is the same as multiplying by 104.5%. The multiplier is 1.045.

$1500 \times 1.045 = £1567.50$
Interest paid = £67.50

If Asif kept his money in the account for three years he would get...
$3 \times 67.50 = £202.50$

So, at the end of the year, Asif has £1702.50 in his account.

Compound Interest

Compound interest is the type of interest where the bank pays interest on interest earned as well as on the original money.

Example

Asif has £1500 in his savings account. Compound interest is earned at 4.5% p.a. How much will Asif have in his account after three years?

Increasing by 4.5% is the same as multiplying by 104.5%. The multiplier is 1.045.

Value of savings...
After 1 year = 1500 × 1.045 = £1567.50
After 2 years = 1567.50 × 1.045 = £1638.04
After 3 years = 1638.04 × 1.045 = £1711.75

A quicker way is to write...
$$1500 \times 1.045 \times 1.045 \times 1.045$$
$$= 1500 \times 1.045^3$$
$$= £1711.75$$

Reverse Percentage Problems

In reverse percentage problems the original quantity is calculated.

Examples

1 The price of a bottle of perfume is reduced by 10%. If it now costs £34.20, what was the original price?

The sale price is...
100% – 10% = 90% of the pre-sale price.

0.9 × (original price) = 34.20

original price = $\dfrac{34.20}{0.9}$

= £38

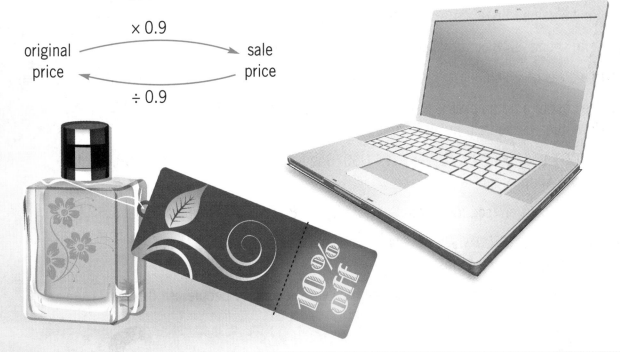

original price $\xrightarrow{\times 0.9}$ sale price

$\xleftarrow{\div 0.9}$

2 The price of a computer is £499 including VAT at 15%. Work out the price of the computer excluding VAT.

The price including VAT...
100% – 15% of the original price.

1.15 × (original price before tax) = the price including VAT

1.15 × (original price before tax) = 499

original price before tax = $\dfrac{499}{1.15}$

= £433.91

Quick Test

1 20% of £60 = 12. True or false?
2 An increase of 45% is represented by which multiplier?
   a) 0.45   **b)** 1.45   **c)** 1.045   **d)** 0.045
3 The simple interest earned per year on £10 000 with an interest rate of 5% is £10 500. True or false?
4 Calculate 25m as a percentage of 2km.

Percentages

Skills Practice

1 Find the new amount when...
  a) £60 is increased by 8%.
  b) £430 is decreased by 9%.
  c) 2.7kg is decreased by 16%.
  d) 33kg is increased by 35%.

2 Erin earns £428 per week working in an office. She is given a pay rise of 2.45%. Work out Erin's new weekly wage.

3 Amelie gained 56 out of 75 in a German test. What percentage did she get?

4 Colin spends £48 out of £136 on rent. What percentage does he spend on rent?

5 In a class of 28 students, 3 students are left-handed. What percentage are left-handed?

6 The cost of a train ticket is £34. The train fares increase by 6% in April. How much is the train ticket in April?

7 In 2001 Lucy bought a flat for £126 000. She sold it for £212 000 in 2008. What is her percentage profit?

8 Sarah bought an ipod for £175. She sold it for £86. What is her percentage loss?

9 A car costs £16 500 when new. Two years later it is sold for £12 150. What is the percentage loss?

10 In a survey of 240 people, 37.5% use the gym. How many people use the gym?

11 A new power saw costs £78. With depreciation its value falls by 12% each year.
Work out the value of the power saw after two years.

12 An investment of £7000 is made for three years at 4% p.a. compound interest.
What is the total interest earned?

13 If £4500 is invested for two years at 5.5% p.a compound interest, what is the total
interest earned?

14 A painting costs £870. Each year it increases in value by 7%.
How much is the painting worth after two years?

15 Audrey bought a train ticket using a senior railcard and was given a reduction of 32%.
She paid £19.04 for her ticket. Calculate the full price of the ticket, before the discount.

16 The cost of a theatre ticket rises by 7% to £23.54.
What was the original price of the ticket?

17 The cost of a washing machine is £424.15 after a 15% reduction.
What was the original cost of the washing machine?

15% off

Standard Index Form

Standard Index Form

Standard index form is used as a simpler way to write very large or very small numbers.

A number written in standard form is written as...

$$a \times 10^n$$

Where $1 \leq a < 10$ and n is the power of 10 (**index**) by which you multiply or divide.

In general...
- the front number (a) must always be at least 1 but less than 10
- the power of 10, n:
  - if the number is large, n is positive
  - if the number is small, n is negative.

Examples
1. The planet Venus is 108 000 000km from the sun. In standard form this is 1.08×10^8km since you move decimal place by eight places.

2. A red corpuscle (blood cell) in a typical adult weighs about 0.000 000 0001 gram. In standard form this is 1×10^{-10} gram.

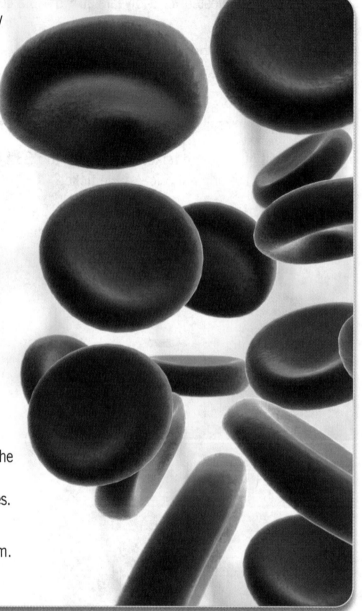

Large Numbers

Use the method below to simplify very large numbers.

Examples
1. Write 7 210 000 in standard index form.
   - Write the number so it lies between 1 and 10. In this case it is 7.21.
   - Work out how many times you multiply by 10 to restore the number (the power of 10). 7.21×10^6

In standard index form 7 210 000 = 7.21×10^6

2. Write 64 000 in standard index form...
   64 000 = 6.4×10^4

Small Numbers

Use the method below to simplify very small numbers.

Examples

1. Write 0.000 546 in standard index form.

   - Write the number so that it lies between 1 and 10. In this case it is 5.46.
   - Work out how many times you divide the number by 10.
     5.46×10^{-4}

     In standard index form
     $0.000\,546 = 5.46 \times 10^{-4}$

2. Write 0.000 000 714 in standard index form...
   $0.000\,000\,714 = 7.14 \times 10^{-7}$

Standard Form and the Calculator

To key a number in standard index form into the calculator, use the EXP key. Some calculators have a EE key – check your calculator.

Examples

1. 7.9×10^{4} is keyed in as

   7 . 9 EXP 4

2. 5.73×10^{-6} is keyed in as

   5 . 7 3 EXP – 6

   The display panel of some calculators doesn't show standard form correctly.

   4.92^{-07} means 4.92×10^{-7}

3. Work out $(7 \times 10^{29}) \times (6 \times 10^{-12})$.
   Leave your answer in standard index form.

   Check you get the answer 4.2×10^{18}

4. Work out $\sqrt{\dfrac{(7.6 \times 10^{12})^2}{(3.1 \times 10^{-4})}}$
   Check you get the answer 4.32×10^{14}.

Standard Index Form

Calculations with Standard Index Form

A calculator can be used to do more complex calculations involving standard index form.

For example...
$(4 \times 10^9) \times (3 \times 10^{-7}) = 1200 = 1.2 \times 10^3$
would be keyed in as...

The laws of indices can also be used when manually multiplying and dividing numbers written in standard form.

Examples

① $(3 \times 10^7) \times (5 \times 10^6)$
   $= (3 \times 5) \times (10^7 \times 10^6)$ ← Add the powers together, $6 + 7 = 13$
   $= 15 \times 10^{13}$
   $= 1.5 \times 10^{14}$

② $(6 \times 10^9) \div (2 \times 10^4)$
   $= (6 \div 2) \times (10^9 \div 10^4)$ ← Subtract the powers, $9 - 4 = 5$
   $= 3 \times 10^5$

Quick Test

1. 270 written in standard form is 2.7×10^2. True or false?
2. 0.0046 written in standard form is 46×10^{-4}. True or false?
3. 3×10^6 written as an ordinary number is...
   a) 3000   b) 30 000   c) 0.000 003
   d) 0.000 000 3
4. $(3 \times 10^5) \times (2 \times 10^7) = 6 \times 10^{35}$. True or false?

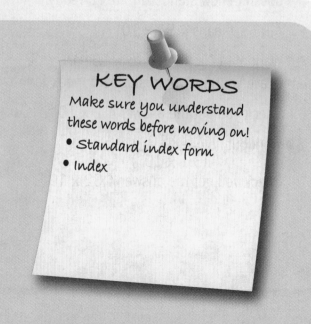

KEY WORDS
Make sure you understand these words before moving on!
- Standard index form
- Index

Skills Practice

1 Write the following in standard form.

a) 7560

b) 3 000 000

c) 520 000

d) 490 000 000

e) 630 000

f) 71 000

g) 5 200 000

h) 41 000

i) 9 800 000

2 Write the following in standard form.

a) 0.004 6

b) 0.000 009

c) 0.097

d) 0.84

e) 0.000 009 1

f) 0.000 099

g) 0.476

h) 0.000 000 000 7

i) 0.000 055 5

3 Write the following numbers as ordinary numbers.

a) 3×10^4

b) 6×10^2

c) 3.2×10^5

d) 7.2×10^7

e) 3.6×10^{-5}

f) 2.5×10^{-3}

g) 6×10^{-2}

h) 5×10^{-4}

i) 7.4×10^{-8}

4 Work out the following without using a calculator.

a) $(2 \times 10^6) \times (4 \times 10^5)$

b) $(3 \times 10^9) \times (1 \times 10^2)$

c) $(4 \times 10^5) \times (2 \times 10^3)$

d) $(6 \times 10^7) \div (3 \times 10^4)$

e) $(8 \times 10^{11}) \div (4 \times 10^6)$

5 Work out the following using a calculator. 🖩

a) $(6 \times 10^9) \times (3 \times 10^5)$

b) $(1.2 \times 10^{10}) \times (2.8 \times 10^9)$

c) $(6 \times 10^{-4}) \times (3 \times 10^8)$

d) $(7 \times 10^{-6}) \times (3 \times 10^{-8})$

e) $(4 \times 10^{-3}) \times (6 \times 10^{10})$

Number Patterns & Sequences

The nth Term of a Linear Sequence

You can find a term in a sequence using a position-to-term rule if you know its position.

This is called a linear sequence because it goes up by a constant amount each time.

Position in Sequence	1	2	3	4	5
Term	6	11	16	21	26

$\times 5 + 1$

$+5 \quad +5 \quad +5 \quad +5$

The term-to-term rule is 'add 5'.

The nth term of a sequence is the same as the position-to-term rule, written using algebra.

For example...

Position in Sequence	1	2	3	4	5	...	n
Term	6	11	16	21	26	...	$5n+1$

$\times 5 + 1$

The position-to-term rule is 'multiply by 5 and add 1'. The nth term would be $5n + 1$.

Position in Sequence	1	2	3	4	5	...	n
Term	4	7	10	13	16	...	$3n+1$

$\times 3 + 1$

$+3 \quad +3 \quad +3 \quad +3$

To find the nth term, look at the gap between the terms. In this example it is 'add 3'. Since the gap is the same it always multiplies with the nth term so $3n$.

Now check: when $n = 1$
$3 \times 1 = 3$, however since the term is 4 we adjust it by adding 1, which gives $3n + 1$.

The nth Term of a Quadratic Sequence

For a quadratic sequence, the first differences are not constant but the second differences are.

The nth term takes the form...
$$an^2 + bn + c$$

Where either b and / or c may be zero.

Example

Find the nth term of 2, 6, 12, 20...

Position in sequence	1	2	3	4	5
Term	2	6	12	20	30
First difference		4	6	8	10
Second difference			2	2	2

a is found by dividing the second difference by 2.
nth term is $n^2 + n$ or $n(n + 1)$

The sequence can be represented by a spatial pattern using rectangles. The areas of these rectangles are:

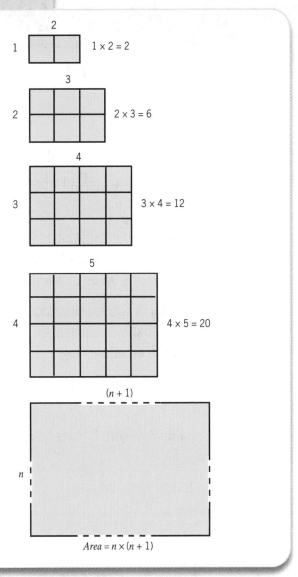

$1 \times 2 = 2$

$2 \times 3 = 6$

$3 \times 4 = 12$

$4 \times 5 = 20$

$Area = n \times (n + 1)$

Quick Test

1 Find the nth term for each of these sequences.

    a) 2, 4, 6, 8, 10,...
    b) 3, 5, 6, 9, 11,...
    c) 4, 6, 8, 10, 12,...
    d) 7, 10, 13, 16, 19,...
    e) 6, 10, 14, 18, 22,...
    f) 9, 8, 7, 6, 5,...
    g) 3, 8, 13, 18, 23,...

2 Find the nth term for each of these sequences.
    a) 1, 4, 9, 16, 25,...
    b) 2, 8, 18, 32, 50,...
    c) 0, 3, 8, 15, 24,...
    d) -2, 1, 6, 13, 22,...
    e) 5, 20, 45, 80, 125...

Working with Algebra

Algebra Terms

Algebra uses letters to represent values.

An **expression** is any arrangement of letters and symbols.

A **formula** connects two expressions containing **variables**. The value of one variable depends on the value of another.

An **equation** connects two expressions, involving definite unknown values. An equation must have an equals sign.

The **identity** connects expressions involving unspecified numbers.

A **function** is a relationship between two sets of variables.

The rules to follow when writing expressions are...

$a + a + a = 3a$

$x \times y \times 3 = 3xy$ ← The number is written first and the letters put into alphabetical order

$x \div 4 = \dfrac{x}{4}$

Laws of Indices

There are laws that apply when working with **indices**.

a^b

b is the index or power

a is the base

The bases in the equation have to be the same when the laws of indices are applied.

To multiply **powers** of numbers or letters, add the indices together, e.g. $x^a \times x^b = x^{a+b}$.

Example
$$y^5 \times y^2 = (y \times y \times y \times y \times y) \times (y \times y)$$
$$= y^7$$

To divide indices of numbers or letters, subtract the indices, e.g. $x^a \div x^b = x^{a-b}$.

Example
$$y^7 \div y^3 = \frac{y \times y \times y \times y \times y \times y \times y}{y \times y \times y}$$
$$= y \times y \times y \times y$$
$$= y^4$$

Cancel $y \times y \times y$ top and bottom

To find the power of a power, multiply the indices together, e.g. $(x^a)^b = x^{a \times b}$.

Example
$$(y^2)^3 = y^2 \times y^2 \times y^2 = y^6$$

Any letter raised to the power of zero is equal to 1, e.g. $a^0 = 1$, $x^0 = 1$, $y^0 = 1$.

Examples
Simplify...

① $2x^5 \times x^4 = 2x^{5+4} = 2x^9$

② $12x^9 \div 3x^4 = 4x^{9-4} = 4x^5$

Divide the numbers as usual $12 \div 3 = 4$

③ $(x^6)^4 = x^{6 \times 4} = x^{24}$

④ $x^0 = 1$

⑤ $\dfrac{x^7 \times 3x^4}{x^5} = \dfrac{3x^{7+4}}{x^5} = \dfrac{3x^{11}}{x^5} = 3x^{11-5} = 3x^6$

Multiplying out Single Brackets

Remember when you're asked to expand an expression that you need to multiply out both **brackets**.

Examples

Expand...

1 $5(x - 3)$
$= 5x - 15$

> Multiply out both brackets. Simplify by collecting like terms.

2 $x(x-6)$
$= x^2 - 6x$

3 $y(2y + 3)$
$= 2y^2 + 3y$

4 $3y(2y - 4)$
$= 6y^2 - 12y$

Expand and **simplify**...

1 $3(x - 2) + 2(x + 1)$
$= 3x - 6 + 2x + 2$
$= 5x - 4$

2 $5(3x - 1) - 2(x - 3)$
$= 15x - 5 - 2x + 6$
$= 13x + 1$

3 $6(x - 5) - (2x - 1)$
$= 6x - 30 - 2x + 1$
$= 4x - 29$

> $-(2x - 1)$ is the same as $-1(2x - 1)$

4 $2(5x - 1) + 3(x - 6)$
$= 10x - 2 + 3x - 18$
$= 13x - 20$

5 $7(3x - 6) - (x - 4)$
$= 21x - 42 - x + 4$
$= 20x - 38$

Factorising Simple Expressions

Factorising is the addition of brackets to an equation by taking out the common factors.

Example

Factorise...

1 $5x + 10$
$= 5(x + 2)$

> The 5 is the highest common factor. The expression in brackets is the number and letter needed so that when multiplied out it returns to the original.

2 $3x - 9$
$= 3(x - 3)$

3 $12x - 4$
$= 4 (3x - 1)$

4 $16 - 8x$
$= 8(2 - x)$

5 $7x - 21$
$= 7(x - 3)$

6 $15x - 25y$
$= 5(3x - 5y)$

7 $20x - 40y$
$= 20(x - 2y)$

8 $30a^2 - 60a$
$= 30a(a - 2)$

9 $5x^2 + 12x$
$= x(5x + 12)$

10 $25a^2 + 15a$
$= 5a(5a + 3)$

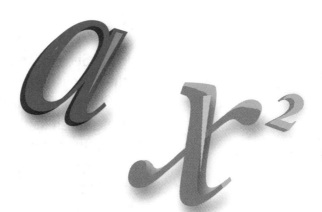

Working with Algebra

Multiplying out Two Brackets

There are several methods that can be used to multiply out two brackets.

Expand $(x + 2)(x + 3)$

Method 1

$(x + 2)(x + 3) = x(x + 3) + 2(x + 3)$

$\qquad\qquad\qquad = x^2 + 3x + 2x + 6$

$\qquad\qquad\qquad = x^2 + 5x + 6$

Multiply out in stages

Simplify by collecting like terms

Method 2

$(x + 2)(x + 3) = x^2 + 3x + 2x + 6$

$\qquad\qquad\qquad = x^2 + 5x + 6$

Multiply each term with each other

Method 3

This rectangle has the lengths $(x + 2)$ and $(x + 3)$. The total area of the rectangle is $(x + 2)(x + 3)$.

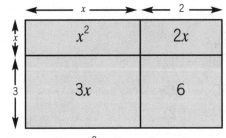

$(x + 2)(x + 3) = x^2 + 3x + 2x + 6$

$\qquad\qquad\qquad = x^2 + 5x + 6$

Examples

Expand…

1 $(x + 3)(x + 5)$

$\quad = x^2 + 5x + 3x + 15$

$\quad = x^2 + 8x + 15$

2 $(x - 1)(x - 4)$

$\quad = x^2 - 4x - x + 4$

$\quad = x^2 - 5x + 4$

3 $(x - 5)(x + 3)$

$\quad = x^2 + 3x - 5x - 15$

$\quad = x^2 - 2x - 15$

4 $(x + 3)(x - 3)$

$\quad = x^2 - 3x + 3x - 9$

$\quad = x^2 - 9$

5 $(x + 3)^2$

$\quad = (x + 3)(x + 3)$

$\quad = x^2 + 3x + 3x + 9$

$\quad = x^2 + 6x + 9$

An expression of the form $ax^2 + bx + c$ is called a **quadratic** expression.

Codes and the Enigma Machine

As long ago as the Ancient Greeks, warring armies have written messages using codes in order to keep their battle plans a secret from their enemies.

Over time the codes and ciphers have become more and more complex and difficult to crack.

During the Second World War, the Germans used the famous Enigma Machine, which they believed to be uncrackable, to encode messages. Polish Mathemeticians worked throughout the pre-war period to try to crack the code. During the war the British worked at Bletchly Park to refine the code breaking and decipher the messages produced using the code.

Factorising Quadratics

You need to be able to factorise a quadratic expression into a pair of **linear** brackets.

Examples

1 Factorise $x^2 + 5x + 6$

> These values multiply to give 6 and add to give 5.

$$x^2 + 5x + 6 = (x \pm a)(x \pm b)$$
$$x^2 + 5x + 6$$
$$= (x + 2)(x + 3)$$

Since $2 \times 3 = 6$ and $2 + 3 = 5$.

2 Factorise $x^2 - 6x + 5$

$$x^2 - 6x + 5$$
$$= (x - 1)(x - 5)$$

Since $-1 \times -5 = 5$ and $-1 - 5 = -6$.

3 Factorise $x^2 - 3x - 4$

$$x^2 - 3x - 4$$
$$= (x + 1)(x - 4)$$

Since $1 \times -4 = -4$ and $1 - 4 = -3$.

4 Factorise $x^2 - 25$

$$x^2 - 25$$
$$= (x - 5)(x + 5)$$

> This is known as the difference of two squares

$5 \times -5 = -25$ and $5 - 5 = 0$ as there is no x term.

In general:

$$x^2 - a^2 = (x + a)(x - a)$$

Substituting into Formulae and Expressions

Remember, you will need to substitute numbers into formulae to solve problems.

Examples

1 If $a = 3$, $b = -2$ and $c = 0.6$, find the value of the expression:

$$a^2 + 2b - 4c$$
$$= 3^2 + (2 \times -2) - (4 \times 0.6)$$
$$= 9 - 4 - 2.4$$
$$= 2.6$$

2 If $p = 4\frac{1}{2}$, $q = 6.5$ and $r = -2$, find the value of the expression:

$$p - 2q^2 + 5r$$
$$= 4\frac{1}{2} - 2 \times (6.5)^2 + (5 \times -2)$$
$$= 4\frac{1}{2} - 84.5 + -10$$
$$= -92$$

3 $V = \frac{4}{3}\pi r^3$ is the formula for a sphere.

Find the value of V if $r = 6.4$cm. Give your answer to 4 s.f.

$$V = \frac{4}{3} \times \pi \times 6.4^3$$
$$V = 1098\text{cm}^3 \text{ (4 s.f.)}$$

Working with Algebra

Rearranging Formulae

The **subject of a formula** is the letter that appears on its own on one side of the formula. Formula can be rearranged to make one of the other letters the subject.

Examples

1 Make y the subject of this formula:

$p = 5y - x$

$p + x = 5y$ ◄ Add x to both sides

$\dfrac{p + x}{5} = y$ ◄ Divide both sides by 5

2 Make b the subject of this formula:

$a = \dfrac{5b^2 - c}{d}$

$ad = 5b^2 - c$ ◄ Multiply both sides by d

$ad + c = 5b^2$ ◄ Add c to both sides

$\dfrac{ad + c}{5} = b^2$ ◄ Divide both sides by 5

$\sqrt{\dfrac{ad + c}{5}} = b$ ◄ Square root both sides

Quick Test

1 $5x^4 \times 3x^6$ simplified is $8x^{10}$. True or false?

2 What does $(x^4)^3$ give?
   a) x^7 **b)** x^{12} **c)** x^1 **d)** x^{16}

3 $5x^2 - 25$ fully factorised is $5(x^2 - 5)$. True or false?

4 Expand and simplify $(x + 2)(x - 6)$

5 $x^2 - 60$ is the difference of two squares. True or false?

KEY WORDS

Make sure you understand these words before moving on!
- Expression
- Formula
- Variable
- Equation
- Identity
- Function
- Indices
- Power
- Brackets
- Expand
- Simplify
- Factorisation
- Quadratic
- Linear
- Difference of two Squares

Skills Practice

1 Simplify...
a) $x^7 \times x^2$
b) $4x \times 3x^2$
c) $10x^4 \div 5x$
d) $(x^4)^5$
e) $20x^6 \div 2x$
f) $12x^7 \div 2x^5$
g) $(2x^2)^3$
h) $(xy)^0$

2 Expand...
a) $7(2x - 1)$
b) $3(x + 6)$
c) $x(3x - 5)$
d) $2x(x + 6)$
e) $(x + 3)(x - 1)$
f) $(x - 7)(x - 2)$
g) $(x + 6)(x + 4)$
h) $(x - 5)(x + 2)$

3 Expand and simplify...
a) $5(x - 6) + 2(x - 1)$
b) $3(2x - 1) + 5(x - 6)$
c) $10(x - 3) + 2(2x - 1)$

4 Factorise...
a) $16x - 12$
b) $20x + 10$
c) $3x^2 + 6x$
d) $12x - 24x^2$
e) $x^2 + 8x + 12$
f) $x^2 + 2x + 1$
g) $x^2 - 7x + 10$
h) $x^2 - 3x - 4$

5 Work out these expressions, if $a = 2$, $b = 7.6$ and $c = -\frac{1}{2}$

a) $a^2 + 2b$
b) $3a - b + 5c$
c) $6a - 3b - c^2$

6 Make t the subject of the formula:
$a^2 = t^2 + d$

Equations & Inequalities

Equations

An **equation** has two parts separated by an equals sign.

When solving an equation, a **solution** to the equation is found.

Solving Equations of the Form $ax + b = c$

Remember, when solving equations of the form $ax + b = c$, to move anything you're adding or subtracting to the other side of the equals sign.

Examples

Solve the following...

1
$$7x - 3 = 10$$
$$7x = 10 + 3$$
$$7x = 13$$
$$x = \frac{13}{7}$$
$$x = 1\frac{6}{7} \quad \longleftarrow \text{Write as a mixed number}$$

2
$$5 - 2x = 10$$
$$5 = 10 + 2x \quad \longleftarrow \text{Subtract } 2x \text{ from both sides to make } 2x \text{ positive}$$
$$5 - 10 = 2x$$
$$-5 = 2x$$
$$-\frac{5}{2} = x$$
$$x = -2.5$$

Solving Equations of the Form $ax + b = cx + d$

Remember, when solving equations of the form $ax + b = cx + d$, to collect all of the letters together on one side of the equals sign and the numbers on the other.

Examples

Solve the following...

1
$$5x - 4 = 3x - 12$$
$$5x - 4 - 3x = -12$$
$$5x - 3x = -12 + 4$$
$$2x = -8$$
$$x = -\frac{8}{2}$$
$$x = -4$$

2
$$\frac{x}{4} + 4 = 2x + 6$$
$$4 = 2x + 6 - \frac{x}{4}$$
$$4 - 6 = 2x - \frac{x}{4}$$
$$-2 = \frac{3x}{4}$$
$$3x = -2 \times 4$$
$$x = -\frac{8}{3}$$

3
$$3(x - 6) = 2(x + 4) \quad \longleftarrow \text{Multiply out the brackets}$$
$$3x - 18 = 2x + 8$$
$$3x - 18 - 2x = 8 \quad \longleftarrow \text{Collect together the } x \text{ values}$$
$$3x - 2x = 8 + 18$$
$$x = 26$$

4
$$5(2x + 1) + 3(x - 2) = 4(2x + 3)$$
$$10x + 5 + 3x - 6 = 8x + 12 \quad \longleftarrow \text{Multiply out the brackets}$$
$$13x - 1 = 8x + 12$$
$$13x - 1 - 8x = 12$$
$$13x - 8x = 12 + 1$$
$$5x = 13$$
$$x = \frac{13}{5}$$
$$x = 2\frac{3}{5}$$

Notice that the answers can be positive, negative, whole or fractional.

Constructing and Solving Linear Equations

Remember to use linear equations to find an unknown value.

Example

A bag contains $b + 3$ green balls, $2b$ blue balls and $3b - 4$ yellow balls. The total number of balls is 35. Form an equation and solve it to find the value of b.

$b + 3 + 2b + 3b - 4 = 35$ ← Form an equation with the information

$$6b - 1 = 35$$
$$6b = 35 + 1$$
$$6b = 36$$
$$b = \frac{36}{6}$$
$$b = 6$$

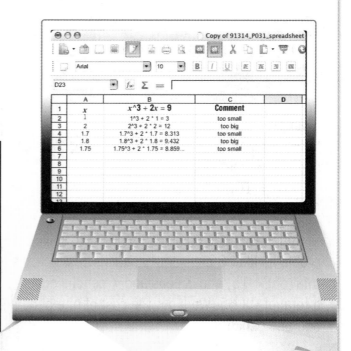

Trial and Improvement

Remember that you can use trial and improvement to get close to a correct value.

Example

The equation $x^3 + 2x = 9$ has a solution between 1 and 2. Use trial and improvement to find the solution. Give your answer correct to one decimal place.

Draw a table to help.

Using spreadsheets is a very useful way of solving equations by trial and improvement, as it's much quicker.

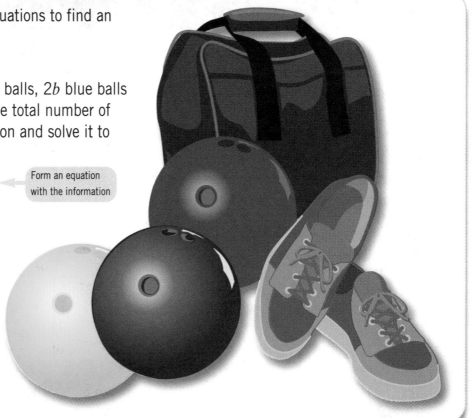

x	$x^3 + 2x = 9$	Comment
1	$1^3 + 2 \times 1 = 3$	too small
2	$2^3 + 2 \times 2 = 12$	too big
1.7	$1.7^3 + 2 \times 1.7 = 8.313$	too small
1.8	$1.8^3 + 2 \times 1.8 = 9.432$	too big
1.75	$1.75^3 + 2 \times 1.75 = 8.859...$	too small

$x = 1.8$ (1 d.p.)

Equations and Inequalities

Simultaneous Equations

You might find that you'll use **simultaneous equations** in your science studies. Simultaneous equations are two equations with two unknown values.

They can be solved in several ways. Solving equations simultaneously involves finding values for the letters which will make both equations work.

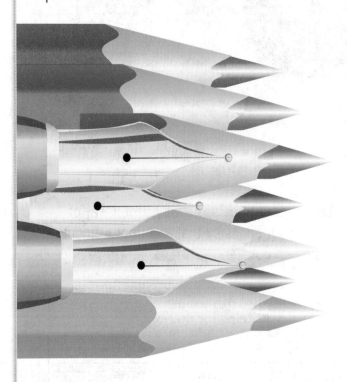

Example

Solve the simultaneous equations using the elimination method.

$2x + 4y = 16$
$3x - y = 3$

Simultaneous equations can be used to solve problems like: 6 pens and 5 pencils cost a total of £4.15, and 3 pens and 7 pencils cost a total of £3.65. Work out the cost of one pen and one pencil.

Try to set up a pair of simultaneous equations and solve them.

Step 1	Label the equations ① and ②
	$2x + 4y = 16$ ①
	$3x - y = 3$ ②
Step 2	Since the **coefficients** don't match, multiply equation ② by 4. Rename it equation ③.
	$2x + 4y = 16$ ①
	$12x - 4y = 3$ ③
	The coefficient is the number a letter is multiplied by, for example, the coefficient of 4y is 4.
Step 3	The coefficient of y in equations ① and ③ are the same. Add equations ① and ③ together to eliminate y and then solve the remaining equation.
	$14x = 28$
	$x = \frac{28}{14}$
	$x = 2$
Step 4	Substitute $x = 2$ into equation ①. Solve the resulting equation to find y.
	$2x + 4y = 16$
	$(2 \times 2) + 4y = 16$
	$4 + 4y = 16$
	$4y = 16 - 4$
	$4y = 12$
	$y = \frac{12}{4}$
	Therefore, $y = 3$
Step 5	Check in equation ②.
	$3x - y = 3$
	$3 \times 2 - 3 = 3$
	The solution is...
	$x = 2, y = 3$

Inequalities

Inequalities can be used when budgeting. It can help to use a computer program that uses inequalities to set a list of conditions that need to be satisfied.

The four inequality symbols are:

>	means greater than
<	means less than
⩽	means greater than or equal to
⩾	means less than or equal to

So, $x > 3$ and $3 < x$ both mean 'x is greater than 3'.

Inequalities are used in an area of mathematics called linear programming. Linear programming was introduced in the 1940s, but has become much more popular since the revolution in the use of computers.

Linear programming is used for solving allocation problems and is widely used in businesses and organisations.

Solving Inequalities

Inequalities are solved in a similar way to equations.

Examples
Solve the inequalities and show the solution set on a number line.

① $2x < 10$

$$x < \frac{10}{2}$$

Divide both sides by 2

$$x < 5$$

When the end point is not included, we use an open circle o.

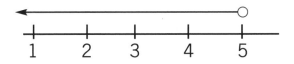

② $5x - 1 \geqslant 14$
$5x \geqslant 14 + 1$
$5x \geqslant 15$
$x \geqslant \frac{15}{5}$
$x \geqslant 3$

When the end point is included, we use a closed circle ●

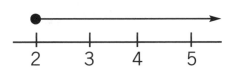

③ $5 \leqslant 6x - 1 < 23$
$6 \leqslant 6x < 24$ ← Add 1 to each part
$1 \leqslant x < 4$ ← Divide each part by 6

The integer values which satisfy this inequality are: 1, 2, 3...

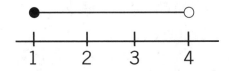

Integers are the set of numbers {...-3, -2, -1, 0, 1, 2, ...}

Equations and Inequalities

Graphical Inequalities

Inequalities can be represented graphically.

The graph of an equation $y = 4$ is a line, whereas the graph of the inequality $y < 4$ is a region that has a line $y = 4$ as its **boundary**.

Example

Leave unshaded the region $x \geq 2$, $y > 1$, $x + y \leq 4$

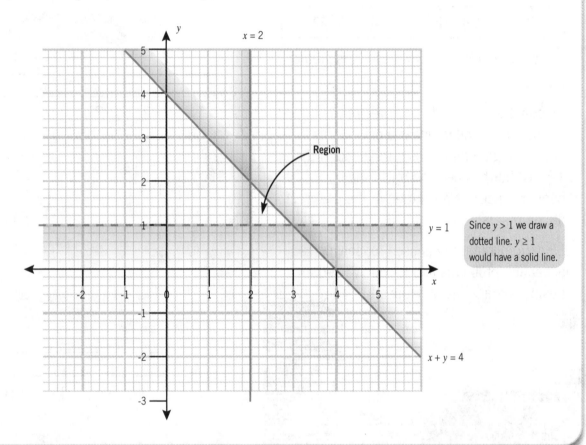

Region

$x = 2$

$y = 1$

Since $y > 1$ we draw a dotted line. $y \geq 1$ would have a solid line.

$x + y = 4$

Quick Test

1. What is the solution to $3x - 1 = 5$?

    a) -2   **b)** $\frac{4}{3}$ **c)** 1   **d)** 2

2. What is the solution to $5(2x - 1) = 30$?

    a) -3   **b)** 3.5   **c)** 2.5   **d)** 3.1

3. The solution to $5x - 1 = 3x + 8$ is $x = 4.5$. True or false?

4. What is the solution to $3(2x - 1) = 2(x + 4)$?

    a) 2.75   **b)** 2.25   **c)** 2.5   **d)** -2.75

KEY WORDS

Make sure you understand these words before moving on!

• Equation
• Solution
• Simultaneous equations
• Coefficients
• Inequalities
• Boundary

Skills Practice

1 Solve the following...

a) $3(x - 6) = 9$

b) $5(2x + 1) = 20$

c) $\dfrac{x}{7} = 4$

d) $\dfrac{3x}{2} + 5 = 11$

e) $4x + 2 = 14$

f) $3x - 5 = 22$

2 Solve the following...

a) $7x - 4 = 3x + 12$

b) $5x - 1 = 2x - 6$

c) $10x - 5 = 4x + 19$

d) $3(x - 6) = 2(2x + 1)$

e) $5(2x + 1) = 2(x - 3)$

f) $4(x - 1) = 3(2x + 6)$

3 Solve the following pairs of simultaneous equations.

a) $x + y = 5$
$x - y = 1$

b) $5x + 2y = 3$
$3x - 2y = 5$

c) $5x + 3y = 4$
$x - y = 4$

4 Solve the following inequalities.
Draw a diagram to show the solution set.

a) $x - 2 \leqslant 9$

b) $3x + 1 > 7$

c) $5x - 2 \leqslant 13$

d) $2 < 2x + 4 \leqslant 16$

5 The equation $y^3 + 2y = 7$ has a solution between
1 and 2. Using the trial and improvement method,
find the solution to the equation. Give your answer
correct to one decimal place.

6 A bag contains $2b$ red balls, $3b - 4$ blue balls and
$6b + 1$ black ball. The total number of balls is 52.
Form an equation and solve it to find the value of b.

Graphs

Drawing Straight Line Graphs

The following are linear (straight line) graphs. Remember that to draw these graphs you need to work out the coordinates of the points to be plotted.

Example
Draw the graphs of...
a) $y = 2x$
b) $y = 2x - 3$
c) $y = 2x + 2$

Method 1
To use a mapping diagram, choose some x coordinates, e.g. -2, 0, 2 and replace x in the function with the given values.

$$y = 2x$$

x	$2x$	Coordinates
-2	$(2 \times -2) = -4$	(-2, -4)
0	$(2 \times 0) = 0$	(0, 0)
2	$(2 \times 2) = 4$	(2, 4)

Method 2
Another method to use would be a table of values.

$$y = 2x$$

x	-2	0	-2
y	-4	0	4

Each value of x is substituted into the equation $y = 2x$, for example,
$x = -2$, $y = 2 \times -2$, $y = -4$.

Plot the set of three coordinates and join them with a straight line and label.

The table of values for the graphs $y = 2x - 3$ and $y = 2x + 2$ are:

$$y = 2x - 3$$

x	-2	0	2
y	-7	-3	1

(-2, -7) (0, -3) (2, 1)

$$y = 2x + 2$$

x	-2	0	2
y	-2	2	6

(-2, -2) (0, 2) (2, 6)

We can see from the graphs below that they all have the same gradient. Depending on the equation, the point where the graph intercepts the y axis will change with each graph.

$y = 2x$ cuts the y axis at (0, 0)

$y = 2x - 3$ cuts the y axis at (0, -3)

$y = 2x + 2$ cuts the y axis at (0, 2)

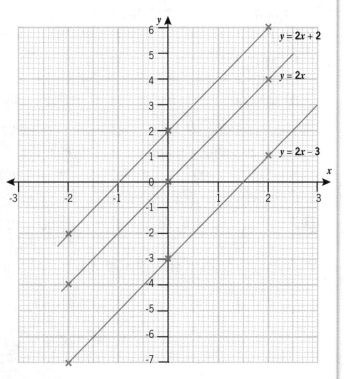

Straight Line Graphs with Different Gradients

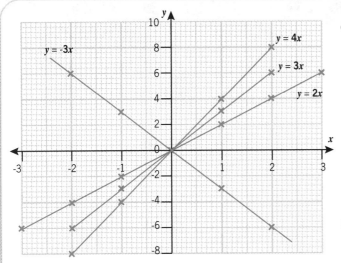

From the graph above we can see that as the number in front of x increases the graph gets steeper.

The number in front of x is called the gradient. The gradient is steeper if the number is bigger.

- A line sloping upwards has a positive gradient.

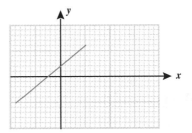

- A line sloping downwards has a negative gradient.

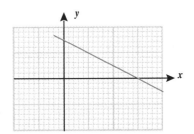

Finding the Gradient of a Straight Line

The general equation of a straight line graph is $y = mx + c$.

m is the gradient and c is the intercept on the y axis.

To find the gradient choose two points that lie on the line.

$$\text{Gradient} = \frac{\text{Change in } y}{\text{Change in } x}$$

Example

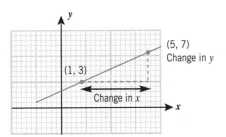

In this example your two points are: (1, 3) and (5, 7).

Use these points to find the change in y (height) and the change in x (base).

$$\text{Gradient} = \frac{\text{Change in } y}{\text{Change in } x} = \frac{\text{Height}}{\text{Base}}$$

$$= \left(\frac{7 - 3}{5 - 1} \right)$$
$$= \frac{4}{4}$$
$$= 1$$

Decide if the gradient is positive or negative.

Graphs

Simultaneous Equations

The point at which two straight line graphs **intersect** (meet) represents the simultaneous solution of their equations.

Example
Solve the **simultaneous equations**:
$y = 3x + 1$
$x + y = 5$

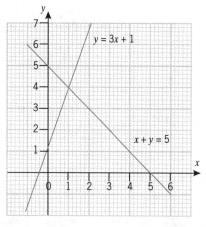

The point of intersection is $x = 1$, $y = 4$. This is the solution of the simultaneous equations.

Highway Code Road Signs

Steep hills are shown using roadsigns.

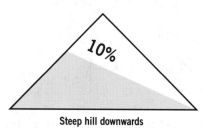

Steep hill downwards

Steep hill upwards

Gradients may be shown as a ratio, for example, 20% = 1 : 5.

Cubic Graphs

When drawing a **cubic graph** of $y = x^3$, it is important to remember that $x^3 = x \times x \times x$.

Example
Draw the graph of $y = x^3$

x	-3	-2	-1	0	1	2	3
y	-27	-8	-1	0	1	8	27

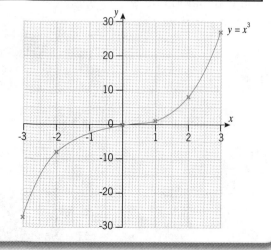

Reciprocal Graphs

The graph of the equation $y = \dfrac{a}{x}$ takes one of two forms, depending on the value of a.

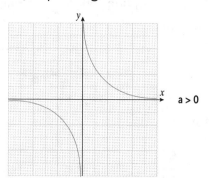

$a > 0$

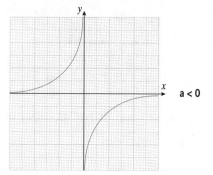

$a < 0$

Quadratic Graphs

Quadratic graphs are graphs of the form $y = ax^2 + bx + c$, where $a = 0$. These graphs are curved.

If the number in front of x^2 is positive, the curve looks like this:

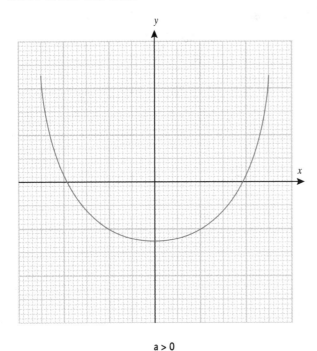

a > 0

If the number in front of x^2 is negative, the curve looks like this:

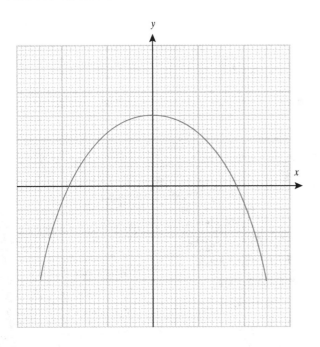

a < 0

Example

Draw the graph of $y = 2x^2 - 5$

Work out a table of values, choosing some values for x.

x	-3	-2	-1	0	1	2	3
y	13	3	-3	-5	-3	3	13

Work out the value of y for each value of x.

When $x = 2$...
$y = 2 \times 2^2 - 5$
$y = 2 \times 4 - 5$
$y = 3$

The coordinates of the points are:
(-3, 13) (-2, 3) (-1, -3) (0, -5) (1, -3) (2, 3) (3, 13)

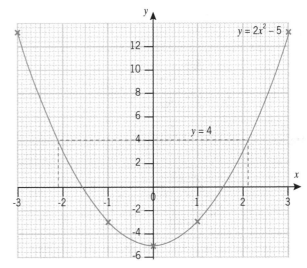

The graph $y = 2x^2 - 5$ has a line of symmetry at $x = 0$. The curve cuts the y axis at (0, -5).

To find the value of x when $y = 4$, read across from $y = 4$ to the graph, then read down to the x axis.

$x = 2.2$ and $x = -2.2$. These are the approximate solutions to $2x^2 - 5 = 4$.

Graphs

Using Graphs

You will find it useful to use graphs in Science and Geography.

Example

These containers are being filled with water at a rate of 100ml per second. The graphs show how the depth of the water changes over time. Match each container with the correct graph.

A

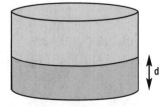

B

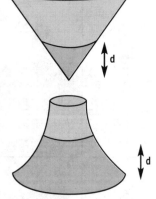

C

Container A
The depth of the water changes uniformly with time.

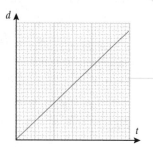

Container B
The depth will rise quickly in the narrow part of the container.

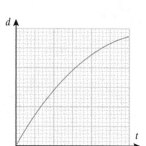

Container C
The depth will increase slowly at the wider part of the container and then increase more quickly at the narrower part.

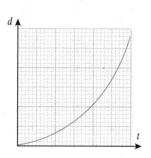

The shape of graphs and their properties can be explored using ICT if you have access to a graphical package.

Quick Test

1. The line $y = 5x - 4$ has a gradient of 4. True or false?
2. The line of $y = 2x + 6$ intercepts the y axis at (0, 6). True or false?
3. $y = x^3$ is a cubic graph. True or false?
4. $y = x^2 - 3$ goes through which coordinate?
   a) (1, 4) **b)** (2, 0) **c)** (3, 5) **d)** (4, 13)

1 a) Draw the graph of...
   i) $y = 4x - 2$
   ii) $y = 2x + 2$

b) Write down the coordinates of the point of intersection.

c) What is the gradient of $y = 4x - 2$?

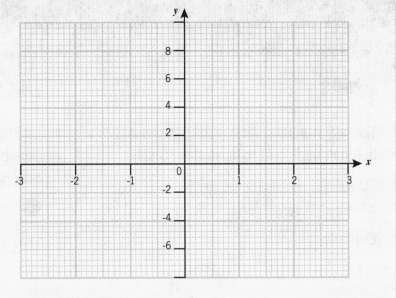

2 From the graph opposite, find the...

a) gradient

b) intercept on the y axis

c) equation of the straight line.

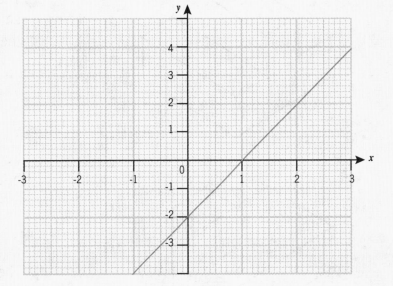

3 a) Draw the graph $y = x^2 - 5$.

b) Write down the equation of the line of symmetry.

c) Using the graph, work out the solution to $x^2 - 5 = 4$.

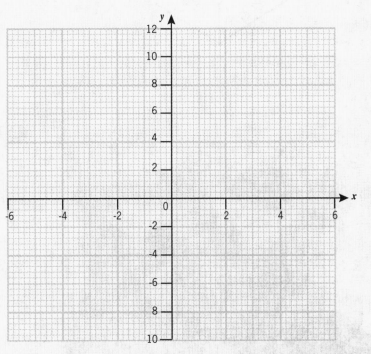

Shapes & Solids

Nets

The **net** of a 3D solid is a 2D flat shape that can be folded to make the 3D solid.

3D solids can be represented on isometric paper.

Examples

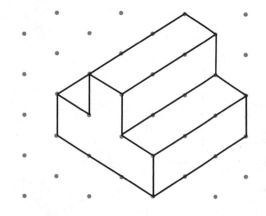

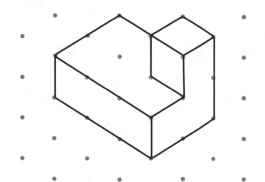

Loci

The **locus** of a point is the set of all the possible positions that point can occupy, subject to some given condition or rule.

1. The locus of the points that are equidistant from a fixed point P is a circle.

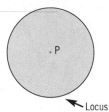

2. The locus of the points that are equidistant from two points X and Y is the perpendicular bisector of XY.

3. The locus of the points that are equidistant from two non-parallel lines is the line that bisects the angle formed by the two lines.

4. The locus of the points that are equidistant from a line is a pair of parallel lines above and below the line.

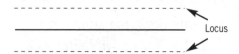

5. The locus of the points that are equidistant from a line segment XY is a pair of parallel lines above and below XY and a semicircle at X and Y.

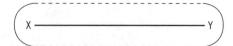

Loci properties can be applied by town and country planners when proposing new developments.

Constructions

To **construct** a regular hexagon inside a circle:

1 Draw a circle with a radius of 2cm, and mark a point *x* on its circumference.

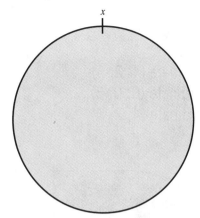

2 Keeping the compass set at 2cm, draw an arc, centre *x* which cuts the circle at *y*. *y* is the centre of the next arc.

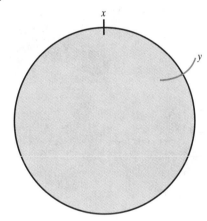

3 Repeat the process until six points are marked on the circumference. Join the points to make a regular hexagon.

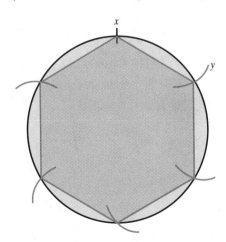

To construct the perpendicular bisector of the line segment XY:

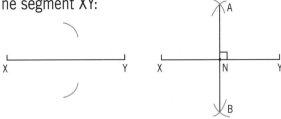

1	Draw two arcs with a compass, using X as the centre.
2	Set the compass at a radius greater than half the length of XY.
3	Draw two more arcs with Y as the centre. (Keep the compasses at the same distance as before.)
4	Join the two points where the arcs cross. AB is the perpendicular bisector of XY. N is the midpoint of XY.

To construct the perpendicular from point P to the line AB:

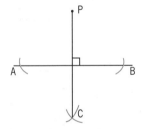

1	From P, draw arcs to cut the line at A and B. From A and B draw arcs with the same radius to intersect at point C below the line.
2	Join P to C; this line is perpendicular to AB.

Using a compass you can construct this triangle.

C

5cm

4cm

B

A

7cm

Not to scale

1	Draw the longest side.
2	With the compass point at A, draw an arc of radius 4cm.
3	With the compass point at B, draw an arc of radius 5cm.
4	Join A and B to the point where the two arcs meet at C.

Shapes & Solids

Coordinates in 3D

The normal $x - y$ coordinates describe a plane. Perpendicular to both of them is a third direction, known as z.

All positions in space have three coordinates (x, y, z).

Example

① For the cuboid below, the vertices have the following coordinates.

O	(0, 0, 0)	**D**	(3, 0, 4)
A	(0, 2, 0)	**E**	(3, 2, 4)
B	(3, 2, 0)	**F**	(0, 2, 4)
C	(3, 0, 0)	**G**	(0, 0, 4)

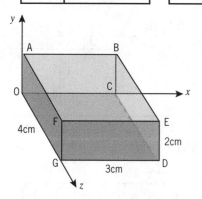

② A has coordinate (4, 2, 5)
B has coordinate (0, 0, 5)
C has coordinate (4, 2, 0)

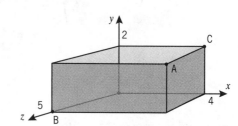

Quick Test

① The locus of the fixed point P is a circle. True or false?
Look at the diagram opposite. Use this diagram to answer Q 2-5.

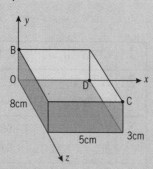

② What are the coordinates of point B?
③ The coordinates of C are (5, 3, 8). True or false?
④ The coordinates of point D are (5, 0, 0). True or false?

ESSENTIALS

Year 9
KS3 Mathematics
Coursebook Answers

NUMBERS

Page 6 – Quick Test

1. $30 \times 40 \div 6 = \frac{120}{6} = 20$

2. a) 2700
   b) 9.6
   c) 2.1

3. True

4. False

Page 7 – Skills Practice

1. a) True
   b) False
   c) True
   d) True
   e) True
   f) False
   h) True

2. a) $900 \times 400 = 360\,000$
   b) $40 \times 20 = 800$
   c) $200 \times 2000 = 400\,000$
   d) $\frac{9000 - 10}{10} = 899$

3. a) 4^7
   b) 3^8
   c) 4^7
   d) 6^5
   e) 10^4
   f) 6^7
   g) 7^3
   h) 8^3

4. a) 6
   b) 22
   c) 8
   d) 5

5. a) $25 = 5 \times 5$
   b) $42 = 2 \times 3 \times 7$
   c) $72 = 2 \times 2 \times 2 \times 3 \times 3$

6. a) HCF = 5, LCM = 180
   b) HCF = 4, LCM = 112
   c) HCF = 4, LCM = 480

7. a) Lower 615, Upper 624
   b) Lower 3545, Upper 3554
   c) Lower 5550, Upper 5649
   d) Lower 156 500, Upper 157 499
   e) Lower 2.65, Upper 2.75

FRACTIONS, DECIMALS & RATIO

Page 10 – Quick Test

1. True

2. £12 000

3. True

4. 6.04, 6.27, 6.37, 6.371, 6.49

Page 11 – Skills Practice

1. a) $\frac{64}{77}$
   b) $\frac{7}{15}$
   c) $5\frac{13}{15}$
   d) $1\frac{7}{9}$

2. a) $\frac{6}{35}$
   b) $8\frac{1}{3}$
   c) $3\frac{27}{40}$
   d) $1\frac{4}{45}$

3. a) $1\frac{5}{7}$
   b) $2\frac{2}{3}$
   c) $\frac{49}{87}$
   d) $1\frac{19}{56}$

4. a) 6.48
   b) 17.24
   c) 25.42
   d) 9.38

5. 20

6. 7.37m, 12.04m, 12.06m, 12.39m, 12.41m, 12.63m

7. 0.0124

8. £16.72

9. 200

PERCENTAGES

Page 15 – Quick Test

1. True

2. b) 1.45

3. False

4. 1.25%

Pages 16–17 – Skills Practice

1. a) £64.80
   b) £391.30
   c) 2.268kg
   d) 44.55kg

2. £438.49

3. 74.6%

4. 35.3%

5. 10.7% (1 d.p.)

6. £36.04

7. 68.3%

8. 50.9% (1 d.p.)

9. 26.4% (1 d.p.)

10. 90

11. £60.40

12. £874.05

13. £508.61

14. £996.06

15. £28

16. £22

17. £499

STANDARD INDEX FORM

Page 20 – Quick Test

1. True

2. True

3. b) 30 000

4. False

Page 21 – Skills Practice

1. a) 7.56×10^3
   b) 3×10^6
   c) 5.2×10^4
   d) 4.9×10^8
   e) 6.3×10^5
   f) 7.1×10^4
   g) 5.2×10^6
   h) 4.1×10^4
   i) 9.8×10^6

2. a) 4.6×10^{-3}
   b) 9×10^{-6}
   c) 9.7×10^{-2}
   d) 8.4×10^{-1}
   e) 9.1×10^{-6}
   f) 9.9×10^{-5}
   g) 4.76×10^{-1}
   h) 7×10^{-10}
   i) 5.55×10^{-5}

3. a) 30 000
   b) 600
   c) 320 000
   d) 72 000 000
   e) 0.000036
   f) 0.0025
   g) 0.06
   h) 0.0005
   i) 0.000000074

4. a) 8×10^{11}
   b) 3×10^{11}
   c) 8×10^8
   d) 2×10^3
   e) 2×10^5

5. a) 1.8×10^{15}
   b) 3.36×10^{19}
   c) 1.8×10^5
   d) 2.1×10^{-13}
   e) 2.4×10^8

NUMBER PATTERNS & SEQUENCES

Page 23 – Quick Test

1. a) $2n$
   b) $2n + 1$
   c) $2n + 2$ or $2(n + 1)$
   d) $3n + 4$
   e) $4n + 2$
   f) $10 - n$
   g) $5n - 2$

2. a) n^2
   b) $2n^2$
   c) $n^2 - 1$
   d) $n^2 - 3$
   e) $5n^2$

WORKING WITH ALGEBRA

Page 28 – Quick Test

1. False

2. b) x^{12}

3. True

4. $x^2 - 4x - 12$

5. False

Page 29 – Skills Practice

1. a) x^9
   b) $12x^3$
   c) $2x^3$
   d) x^{20}
   e) $10x^5$
   f) $6x^2$
   g) $8x^6$
   h) 1

2. a) $14x - 7$
   b) $3x + 8$
   c) $3x^2 - 5x$
   d) $2x^2 + 12x$
   e) $x^2 + 2x - 3$
   f) $x^2 - 9x + 14$
   g) $x^2 + 10x + 24$
   h) $x^2 - 3x - 10$

3. a) $7x - 32$
   b) $11x - 33$
   c) $14x - 32$

4. a) $4(4x - 3)$
   b) $10(2x + 1)$
   c) $3x(x + 2)$
   d) $12x(1 - 2x)$
   e) $(x + 2)(x + 6)$
   f) $(x + 1)(x + 1)$
   g) $(x - 2)(x - 5)$
   h) $(x + 1)(x - 4)$

5. a) 19.2
   b) -4.1

c) -11.05

6. $t = \sqrt{a^2 - d}$

EQUATIONS & INEQUALITIES

Page 34 – Quick Test

1. d) 2

2. b) 3.5

3. True

4. a) 2.75

Page 35 – Skills Practice

1. a) $x = 9$
   b) $x = 1.5$
   c) $x = 28$
   d) $x = 4$
   e) $x = 3$
   f) $x = 9$

2. a) $x = 4$
   b) $x = \frac{-5}{3}$
   c) $x = 4$
   d) $x = -20$
   e) $x = -1\frac{3}{8}$
   f) $x = -11$

3. a) $x = 3, y = 2$
   b) $x = 1, y = -1$
   c) $x = 2, y = -2$

4. a) $x \leq 11$

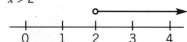

b) $x > 2$

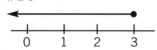

c) $x \leq 3$

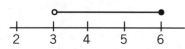

d) $3 < x \leq 6$

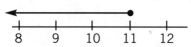

5. $x = 1.6$ (1 d.p.)

6. $b = 5$

GRAPHS

Page 40 – Quick Test

1. False

2. True

3. True

4. d) (4, 13)

Page 41 – Skills Practice

1. a) i) and ii)

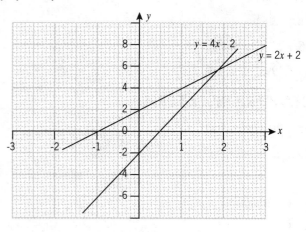

b) (2 , 6)
c) 4

2. a) Gradient = 2
   b) (0 , 2)
   c) $y = 2x - 2$

3. a)

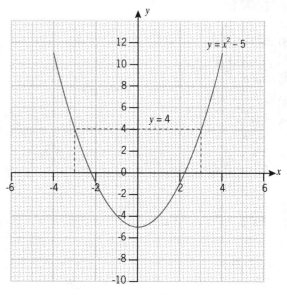

b) $y = 0$
c) $x = 3$ or $x = -3$

SHAPES & SOLIDS

Page 44 – Quick Test

1. True

2. (0, 3, 0)

3. False

4. True

Page 45 – Skills Practice

1.

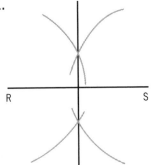

2.

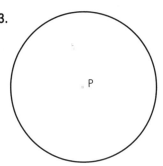

3.

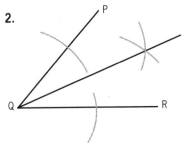

4. P (0, 2, 0)
    Q (0, 1, 7)
    R (4, 1, 7)
    S (1, 2, 6)
    T (0, 1, 6)

ANGLES & COMPOUND MEASURES

Page 49 – Quick Test

1. $47°$

2. False

3. 175 miles

4. 72mph

Pages 50–51 – Skills Practice

1. a) $a = 68°$
    $b = 68°$
    $c = 68°$
    $d = 112°$
  b) $a = 55°$
    $b = 75°$
  c) $a = 52°$
    $b = 76°$
  d) $a = 98°$
  e) $a = 89°$
    $b = 91°$

    $c = 91°$
    $d = 91°$
  f) $a = 113°$

2. Exterior angle = $45°$
    Interior angle = $135°$

3. $30°$

4. a) i) $065°$
    ii) $245°$
  b) i) $135°$
    ii) $315°$
  c) i) $327°$
    ii) $147°$

5. a) i) $320°$
    ii) $140°$
  b) i) $143°$
    ii) $323°$
  c) i) $233°$
    ii) $053°$

6. 170km

7. $0.09\dot{3}$kg/m^3

8. 112.5km/h

9. 7.8g

PERIMETER, AREA & VOLUME

Page 54 – Quick Test

1. True

2. 69.12cm (2 d.p.)

3. True

Page 55 – Skills Practice

1. 165cm^2

2. 7.96cm (2 d.p.)

3. a) 67.5cm^3
  b) 240cm^3
  c) 1592.79cm^3

4. a) 114cm^2
  b) 288cm^2
  c) 755.55cm^2

5. Volume = 150cm^3
    Surface Area = 218cm^2

6. a) 60 000cm^2
  b) 5 000 000cm^3
  c) 160 000cm^2
  d) 40 000mm^3

TRANSFORMATIONS

Page 58 – Quick Test

1. True

2. True

3. False

4.

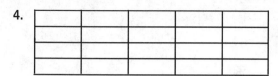

Page 59 – Skills Practice

1. a) – d)

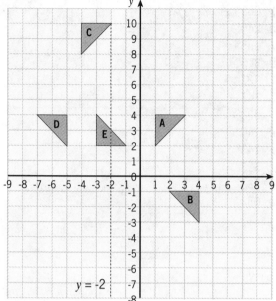

2.

3. a) No – since all three lengths must be the same.
   b) Yes – since two angles and a side are equal.

PYTHAGORAS' THEOREM

Page 62 – Quick Test

1. True

2. It is always opposite the right angle.

3. d) 5 cm

4. True

Page 63 – Skills Practice

1. a) 8.1cm
   b) 19.2m
   c) 11.7m
   d) 37.5m
   e) 76.9m
   f) 55.2m
   g) 9.6m
   h) 31.3m

2. a) 14.7m
   b) 15.7m
   c) 34.4m
   d) 9.7m
   e) 24.4m

   f) 10.5m
   g) 6.5m
   h) 27cm

3. 15cm

4. 20.3cm

SIMILARITY

Page 65 – Skills Practice

1. a) 9.6cm
   b) 20.2cm
   c) 5.1cm
   d) 6.6cm
   e) 10.3cm

2. a) Similar
   b) Similar
   c) Not similar
   d) Similar
   e) Not similar

TRIGONOMETRY

Page 68 – Quick Test

1. b) Opposite

2. True

3. Sine

4. 6m

Page 69 – Skills Practice

1. a) 10.04m
   b) 17.79m
   c) 21.43m
   d) 18.54m
   e) 19.56m
   f) 7.8m

2. a) 36.9°
   b) 36.9°
   c) 37.7°
   d) 43.8°
   e) 41.8°
   f) 30.96° = 31.0° (3 s.f.)

3. 35.7m

4. 33.7°

HANDLING DATA

Page 72 – Quick Test

1. True

2. Negative correlation

3. True

Page 73 – Skills Practice

1. Her results will be biased as most of the people she will ask will use the leisure centre. Her sample also needs to include people who may not use the leisure centre. Also, on a Tuesday morning she will bias her sample towards people who don't work.

2.

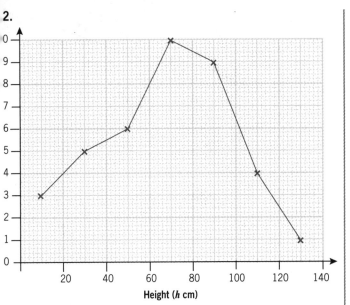

3.

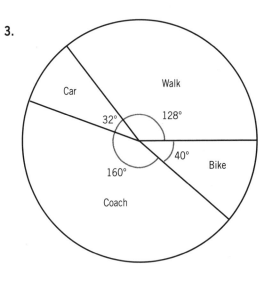

AVERAGES

Page 75 – Quick Test

1. a) 1.214

   b) False

   c) True

   d) False

Pages 76–77 – Skills Practice

1. a) 1.3̇ minutes

   b) 0 minutes

   c) 0 minutes

   d) 6 minutes

2. a) 140.1cm

   b) $135 \leqslant h < 140$

   c) $135 \leqslant h < 140$

3. a) 52.67kg

   b) $50 \leqslant w < 60$

   c) $50 \leqslant w < 60$

4. a) $40 < t \leqslant 60$

   b) 42.3̇ minutes

CUMULATIVE FREQUENCY GRAPHS

Page 80 – Quick Test

1. a) Class T

   b) 67 marks

   c) False

   d) False

Page 81 – Skills Practice

1. a)

Distance (d km)	Frequency	Cumulative Frequency
$0 \leqslant d < 5$	8	8
$5 \leqslant d < 10$	22	30
$10 \leqslant d < 15$	25	55
$15 \leqslant d < 20$	18	73
$20 \leqslant d < 25$	14	87
$25 \leqslant d < 30$	3	90

b)

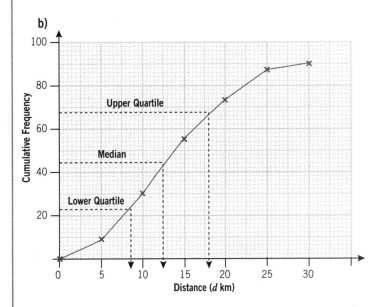

c) Approximately 12.5km

d) Approximately 9.6km

e)

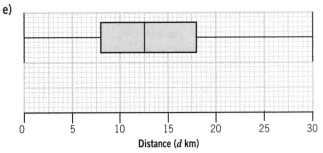

PROBABILITY

Page 85 – Quick Test

1. c) 0

2. $\frac{5}{9}$

3. 250

4. False

Page 86 – Skills Practice

1. a) $\frac{6}{11}$

   b) $\frac{2}{11}$

   c) $\frac{8}{11}$

   d) $\frac{9}{11}$

2. 0.85

3. 0.58

4. $\frac{1}{3}$ or $\frac{2}{6}$

5. 50 times

6. a) 0.3

   b) 20

7. a)

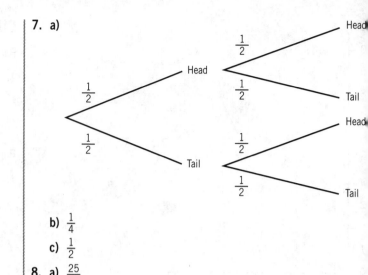

   b) $\frac{1}{4}$

   c) $\frac{1}{2}$

8. a) $\frac{25}{81}$

   b) $\frac{40}{81}$

ACKNOWLEDGEMENTS

The author and publisher are grateful to the copyright holders for permission to use quoted materials and images.

Every effort has been made to trace copyright holders and obtain their permission for the use of copyright material. The authors and publishers will gladly receive information enabling them to rectify any error or omission in subsequent editions. All facts are correct at time of going to press.

Lonsdale
4 Grosvenor Place
London SW1X 7DL

Orders: 015395 64910
Enquiries: 015395 65921
Email: enquiries@lettsandlonsdale.co.uk
Website: www.lettsandlonsdale.com

ISBN: 978-1-844191-31-4

01/290509

Published by Lonsdale

© 2009 Lonsdale, a division of Huveaux Plc.

British Library Cataloguing in Publication Data.

A CIP record of this book is available from the British Library.

Book concept and development: Helen Jacobs
Commissioning Editor: Rebecca Skinner
Author: Fiona Mapp
Project Editor: Emma Rae
Cover Design: Angela English
Inside Concept Design: Helen Jacobs and Sarah Duxbury
Text Design and Layout: Nicola Lancashire
Artwork: Lonsdale

Printed and bound in Italy

Lonsdale make every effort to ensure that all paper used in our books is made from wood pulp obtained from well-managed forests, controlled sources and recycled wood or fibre.

Skills Practice

1 Draw a perpendicular bisector on the line RS.

R ——————————————————— S

2 Bisect the angle PQR.

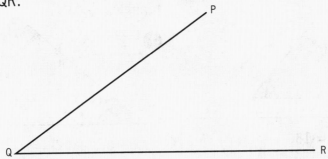

3 On the diagram, draw the locus of the points 4cm from point P.

•P

4 Write down the coordinates of...
P
Q
R
S
T

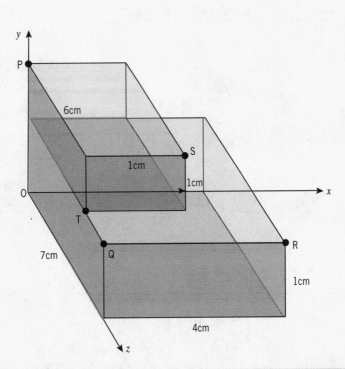

Angles & Compound Measures

Angles in a Triangle

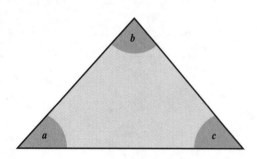

$$a + b + c = 180°$$

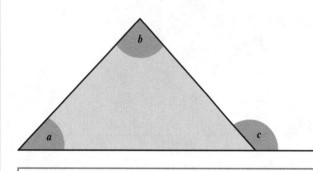

$$a + b = c$$

Examples

Work out the size of **angle** x in each of these triangles.

1

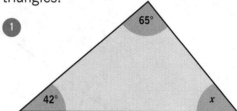

$$x + 63° + 42° = 180°$$
$$x + 105° = 180°$$
$$x = 180° - 105°$$
$$x = 75°$$

2

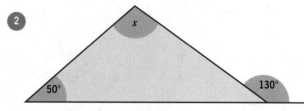

$$x + 50° = 130°$$
$$x = 130° - 50°$$
$$x = 80°$$

Angles in a Quadrilateral

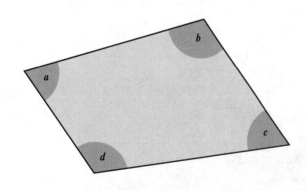

$$a + b + c + d = 360°$$

Example

Find the missing angle in this **quadrilateral**.

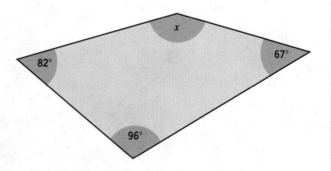

$$x + 82° + 96° + 67° = 360°$$
$$x + 240° = 360°$$
$$x = 360° - 245°$$
$$x = 115°$$

Angles in a Polygon

For a regular **polygon** the sum of the **exterior angles** adds up to 360°.

For 'n' exterior angels, size of an exterior angle	$=$	$\dfrac{360°}{n}$

Interior angle	$+$	exterior angle	$=$	180°

Sum of the interior angles $= (n-2) \times 180°$ or $(2n-4) \times 90°$

Example

A regular polygon has 12 sides. What is the size of the **interior angles**?

$n = 12$ so the exterior angles $= \dfrac{360°}{12}$

Since exterior angle + interior angle = 180°

$$\text{Interior angle} = 180° - 30°$$
$$= 150°$$

Angles in Parallel Lines

Alternate angles: $a = b$

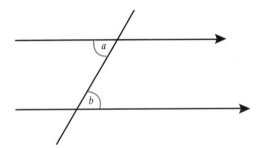

Corresponding angles: $c = d$

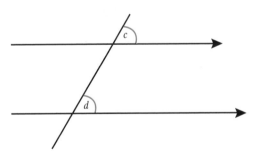

Supplementary angles: $e + f = 180°$

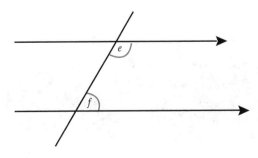

Examples

Find the angles labelled with letters in the diagrams below.

1

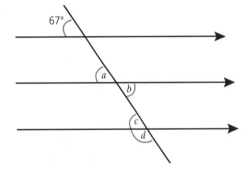

$a = 67°$ (corresponding angles)
$b = 67°$ (opposite to a)
$c = 67°$ (corresponding to 67°)
$d = 113°$ (angles on a straight line)

2

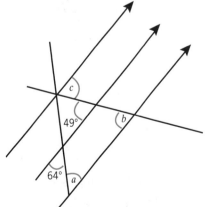

$a = 64°$ (alternate)
$b = 49°$ (corresponding)
$c = 49°$ (corresponding)

Angles & Compound Measures

Bearings

Bearings are always written in three figures and measured from the North line in a clockwise direction.

Example

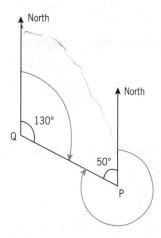

The bearing of P from Q is 130°.
The bearing of Q from P is
360° − 50° = 310°

2️⃣ A ship sails 20km due North and then 25km on a bearing of 075°. Using a scale of 1cm = 5cm, draw an accurate scale drawing of the ship's journey.

N.B. Diagram not drawn to scale

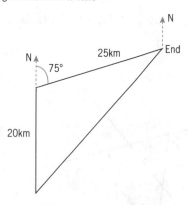

How far and on what bearing is the ship from its starting point?

Distance: 7.3cm = 7.3 × 5
= 36.5km
Bearing = 041°

Compound Measures

Speed can be measured in kilometres per hour (km/h), miles per hour (mph), and metres per second (m/s). These are all compound measures because they involve a combination of basic measures.

To calculate speed...

$$\text{average speed}(s) = \frac{\text{total distance travelled}(d)}{\text{total time taken}(t)}$$

$s = \dfrac{d}{t}$, $t = \dfrac{d}{s}$ and $d = s \times t$

$$\frac{D}{S \times T}$$

Examples

1️⃣ A car travels at 60 km/h for three and a half hours. Find the distance travelled in km.

$s = \dfrac{d}{t}$, so $d = s \times t$

$d = 60 \times 3.5$

$= 210$km.

2️⃣ A car travels 50km in 40 minutes. Work out the average speed in km/h.

$s = \dfrac{d}{t}$ ← 40 minutes needs to be written as a fraction of one hour

$\dfrac{40}{60} = \dfrac{2}{3}$ hour

$s = \dfrac{50}{\frac{2}{3}}$

$= 75$km/h

Concorde

Concordes were the fastest commercial aeroplanes built. A Concorde took off at a speed of 250mph and cruised at a speed of 1350mph, which is more than twice the speed of sound.

Density

Density = $\dfrac{\text{Mass}}{\text{Volume}}$

$$D = \frac{M}{V}$$

so $M = D \times V$ or $V = \dfrac{M}{D}$

Example

Find the density of an object of mass 600g and volume 50cm³.

$$D = \frac{M}{V} = \frac{M}{V} = \frac{600}{50} = 12\text{g/cm}^3$$

Quick Test

1. Two angles in a triangle are 102° and 31°. What is the size of the third angle?
2. Bearings are measured from the north in an anticlockwise direction. True or false?
3. A car travels at 70 mph for two and a half hours. How far has the car travelled?
4. A car travels 120 miles in 1 hour and 40 minutes. What is the speed of the car in mph?

Angles & Compound Measures

1. Work out the size of the missing angles:

a)

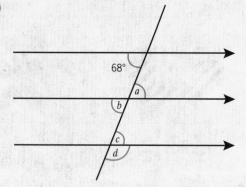

d)

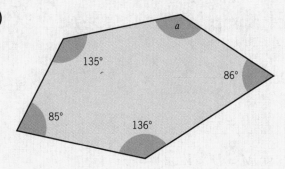

b)

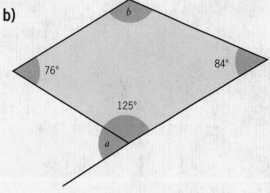

e)

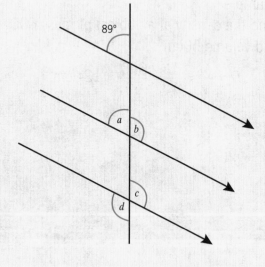

c)

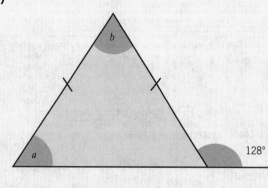

f)

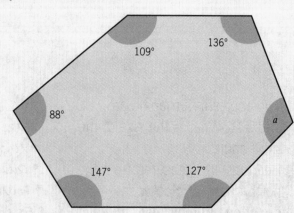

2. Work out the size of the interior and exterior angles of a regular octagon.

3. Work out the size of an exterior angle of a regular shape with 12 sides.

4 For the following, work out...
    i) the bearing of A from B
    ii) the bearing of B from A.

a)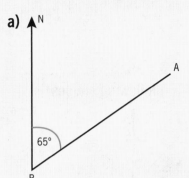

b)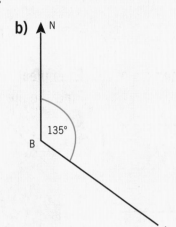

c)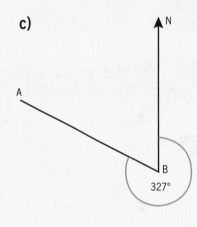

5 For the following, work out...
    i) the bearing of P from Q
    ii) the bearing of Q from P

a)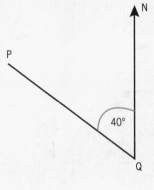

b)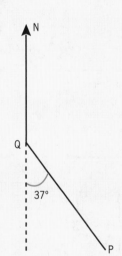

c)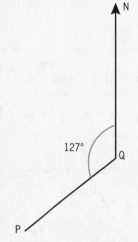

6 A car travels at 85km/h for 2 hours. Find the distance travelled in kilometres.

7 Find the density of an object of mass 7kg and volume 75m^3.

8 A car travels 75km in 40 minutes. What is the speed of the car? 🖩

9 The density of an object is 0.65 kg/cm^3. The volume of the object is 12g. 🖩
What is the mass of the object?

Area & Volume

Area Formulae

There are formulae for calculating the **area** of 2D shapes.

Area of Parallelogram	=	base	✗	perpendicular height

$$A = b \times h$$

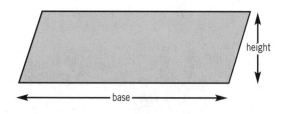

height

base

Area of Trapezium	$= \frac{1}{2} \times$	sum of parallel sides	✗	perpendicular distance between them

$$A = \frac{1}{2} \times (a + b) \times h$$

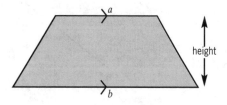

a

height

b

Examples

Find the area of the following shapes.

1

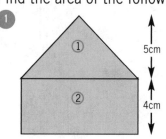

5cm

4cm

7cm

Split into two shapes, ① and ②.

a) $A = \frac{1}{2} \times b \times h$

$\quad\quad = \frac{1}{2} \times 7 \times 5 = 17.5\text{cm}^2$

b) $A = b \times h = 7 \times 4 = 28\text{cm}^2$

Total $= 28 + 17.5$

$\quad A = 45.5\text{cm}^2$

2

7cm

6.3cm

11cm

$A = \frac{1}{2} \times (a + b) \times h$

$\quad = \frac{1}{2} \times (7 + 11) \times 6.3$

$A = 28.35\text{cm}^2$

Volume of a Solid

The **volume** of an object is the amount of space it occupies. Units of volume include mm^3, cm^3, m^3, etc.

A **prism** is a 3D solid. No matter where you cut, it has a constant cross sectional area.

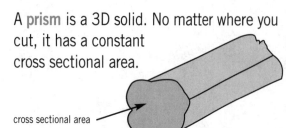

cross sectional area

Volume of a Cuboid

Volume	=	Length	✗	Width	✗	Height

$$V = l \times w \times h$$

To find the **surface area** of a cuboid, find the area of each face.

$$SA = 2hl + 2hw + 2lw$$

Volume of a Prism

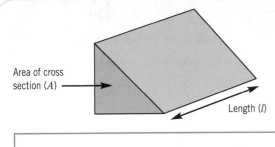

Area of cross section (A)

Length (l)

| Volume | = | Area of a cross section | × | Length |

$$V = A \times l$$

Circles

Circumference
The equation for circumference uses the diameter or radius:

| $C = \pi \times$ diameter | or | $C = \pi \times 2 \times$ radius |

This can be written as:

| $C = \pi d$ | or | $C = 2\pi r$ |

π is usually used to two or three decimal places, π = 3.241 (3 d.p.) or the π button on the calculator can be used.

Area
The equation for area is:

| Area | = | π | × | Radius² |

This is written as:

| $A = \pi r^2$ |

Example
Find the circumference and area of this circle.

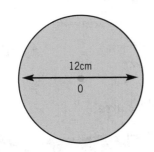

12cm

0

$C = \pi d$
$C = \pi \times 12$
$C = 37.7$cm

$A = \pi r^2$
$A = \pi \times 6^2$
$A = 113.04$cm²

Cylinders

A cylinder is a prism.

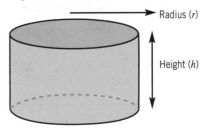

Radius (r)

Height (h)

To work out the volume...

$$V = \pi r^2 \times h$$

area of cross section   height

To work out the surface area...

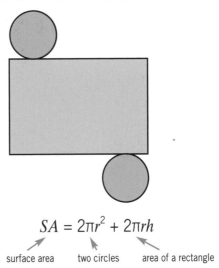

$$SA = 2\pi r^2 + 2\pi rh$$

surface area   two circles   area of a rectangle

When finding the surface area, draw the net of the solid and work out the area of each face.

Example
Work out the volume and surface area of this cylinder.

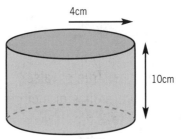

4cm

10cm

Volume $= \pi r^2 h$
$\quad\quad = \pi \times 4^2 \times 10$
$\quad\quad = 502.65$cm³ (2d.p.)

Surface $= 2\pi r^2 + 2\pi rh$
Area $\quad = (2 \times \pi \times 4^2) + (2 \times \pi \times 4 \times 10)$
$\quad\quad = 351.86$cm²

Area & Volume

Converting Units of Area and Volume

$1cm^2$	$= 10 \times 10 = 100mm^2$
$1m^2$	$= 100 \times 100 = 10\,000cm^2$
$1cm^3$	$= 10 \times 10 \times 10 = 1000mm^3$
$1m^3$	$= 100 \times 100 \times 100 = 1000\,000cm^3$

Examples

1 $6m^2 = 6 \times 10\,000$
$\qquad = 60\,000cm^2$

2 $5cm^3 = 5 \times 1000$
$\qquad\quad = 5000mm^3$

Quick Test

1 mm^2 is a unit of area. True or false?
2 Work out the circumference of a circle 🖩 of diameter 22cm, to 2 d.p.
3 The volume of the cylinder below 🖩 is $763m^3$ (nearest whole number). True or false?

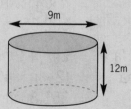

9m

12m

1 Work out the area of the shape below.

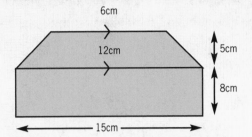

6cm
12cm
5cm
8cm
15cm

2 A circle has a circumference of 50m. Work out its radius to 2 d.p.

3 Work out the **volume** of these solids.

a)
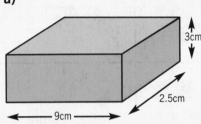
3cm
9cm
2.5cm

b)
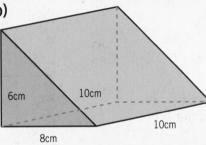
6cm   10cm
8cm   10cm

c)
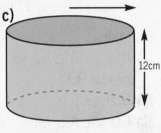
6.5cm
12cm

4 Work out the **surface area** of these solids.

a)
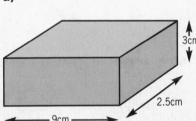
3cm
9cm
2.5cm

b)
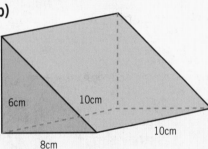
6cm   10cm
8cm   10cm

c)
6.5cm
12cm

5 Work out the volume and surface area of the solid below.

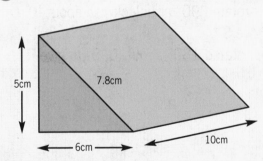
5cm
7.8cm
6cm   10cm

6 Change the following measurements to the units given.

a) $6cm^2$ = _____ m^2

b) $5m^3$ = _____ cm^3

c) $16m^2$ = _____ cm^2

d) $4cm^3$ = _____ m^3

Transformations

Translations and Reflections

Vectors can be used to describe the distance and direction of a **translation**. The vector is written as $\binom{a}{b}$, where a represents the horizontal movement and b represents the vertical movement.

A **reflection** creates an image of an object on the other side of a mirror line (the axis of reflection).

Examples

1. Triangle A is translated by the vector $\binom{-3}{-4}$ to give B.
2. Triangle A is translated by $\binom{4}{-6}$ to give C.
3. Triangle A is reflected in the line $x = 3$ to give D.
4. Triangle A is reflected in the line $y = -x$ to give E.

Triangles B, C, D and E are all **congruent** to A.

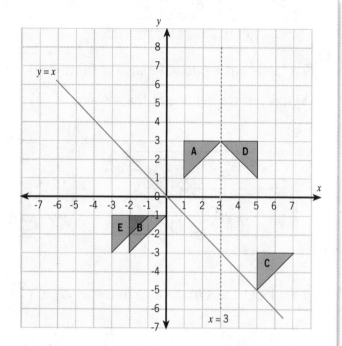

Rotations

A **rotation** turns a figure through a centre of rotation (a fixed point).

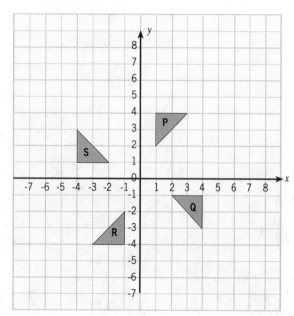

1. P is rotated 90° clockwise about (0, 0) to give Q.
2. P is rotated 90° anticlockwise about (0, 0) to give S.
3. P is rotated 180° about (0, 0) to give R.

Enlargements

The point from which an enlargement takes place is the **centre of enlargement.**

The increase in length is indicated by the **scale factor:**

- Greater than 1 and the shape becomes larger.
- Less than 1 and the shape becomes smaller.

A negative scale factor puts the image on the opposite side of the centre of enlargement to the object.

Examples

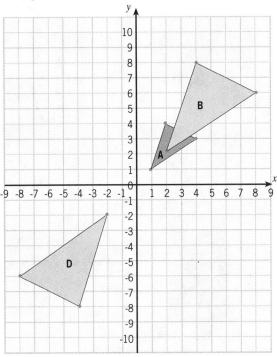

1. B is an enlargement of A, scale factor 2, centre (0, 0).
2. D is an enlargement of A, scale factor -2, centre (0, 0).

Congruent Triangles

Two triangles are congruent if one of the following sets of conditions is true.

S = side, A = angle, R = right angle, H = hypotenuse

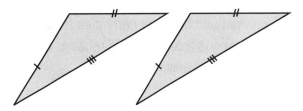

SSS The three sides of one triangle are the same lengths as three sides of another.

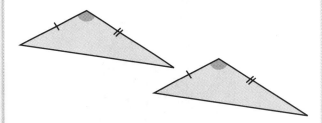

SAS Two sides and the angle between them in one triangle are equal to two sides and the included angle in the other.

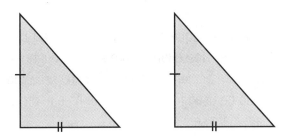

RHS Each triangle contains a right angle. The hypotenuse and the other pair of sides are equal.

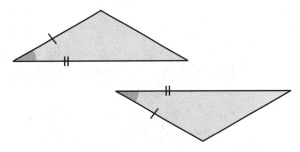

AAS Two angles and a side in one triangle are equal to the two corresponding angles and the corresponding side in the other.

Transformations

Tessellations

Transformation of objects can make **tessellations**. A tessellation is a pattern of 2D shapes that fit together without leaving any gaps.

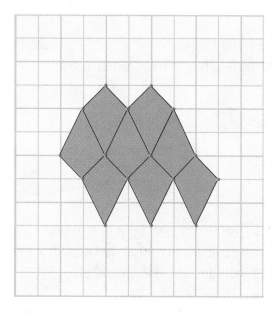

Tessellations frequently appeared in the art of M.C. Escher. Tessellations are seen throughout art history from ancient to modern art. Tessellations can also be used in computer graphics in order to manage data sets of polygons.

Quick Test

1. If a shape is enlarged by a scale factor 3, each length is three times the size of the original. True or false?
2. Two triangles are congruent if all three sides are the same length. True or false?
3. A translation by a vector $\begin{pmatrix} -6 \\ 9 \end{pmatrix}$ means 6 to the right and 9 up. True or false?
4. Rectangles can tessellate. Draw a sketch of tessellated rectangles.

KEY WORDS

Make sure you understand these words before moving on!

- Vector
- Translation
- Reflection
- Congruent
- Rotation
- Centre of enlargement
- Scale factor
- Transformation
- Tessellation

1 For triangle A, carry out the following transformations.

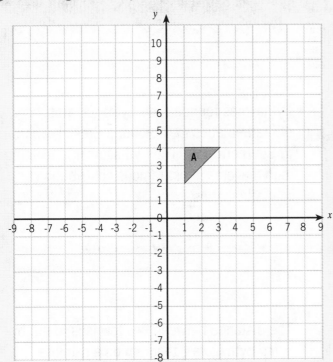

a) Rotate A about (0, 0) by a 90° clockwise rotation. Call the shape B.

b) Translate A by the vector $\begin{pmatrix} -5 \\ 6 \end{pmatrix}$. Call the shape C.

c) Reflect A in the line $y = -2$. Call the shape D.

d) Rotate A by 90° anticlockwise about the point (0, 1). Call the shape E.

2 Continue the tessellation below. Draw at least six more shapes.

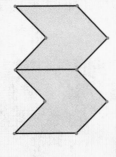

3 Decide whether these pairs of triangles are congruent, giving a reason for your answer.

a)

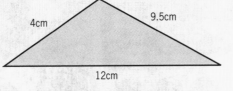

4cm 9.5cm 9.3cm 4cm 12cm 12cm

b)

15cm 37° 101° 101° 42° 15cm

Pythagoras' Theorem

Pythagoras

Pythagoras, a Greek philosopher and mathematician, was born about 570 BC in Samos, Ionia, and died about 490 BC. Much of his work was said to have been influenced by the philosopher and mathematician Plato.

Pythagoras founded the Pythagorean school of mathematics in Crotone, a Greek seaport in Southern Italy. The Pythagorean Theorem is Pythagoras' most famous contribution to mathematics.

Pythagoras' Theorem

Pythagoras' Theorem states: 'In any right angled triangle, the square of the hypotenuse is equal to the sum of the squares on the other two sides.'

The hypotenuse is the longest side of a right angled triangle; it is always opposite the right angle.

The distance between two towns is found by using pythagoras' theorem on a satellite navigation system.

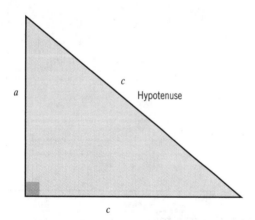

Using the letters in the diagram, the theorem is written as:

$$c^2 = a^2 + b^2$$

This can be rearranged as:
$$a^2 = c^2 - b^2 \text{ or } b^2 = c^2 - a^2$$

This will help you to find the length of one of the shorter sides.

Finding the Length of the Hypotenuse

You need to follow the steps below to find the hypotenuse of a right angled triangle.

Examples

1 Find the length AB in the triangle below. Give your answer to one decimal place.

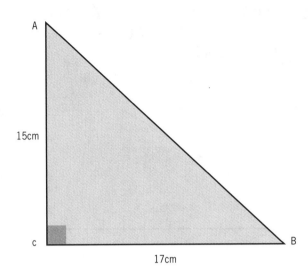

- Square the two lengths of the shorter sides that you are given.
$$(AB)^2 = (AC)^2 + (BC)^2$$
$$= 15^2 + 17^2$$

- To find the hypotenuse, add the two squared numbers.
$$(AB)^2 = (AC)^2 + (BC)^2$$
$$= 15^2 + 17^2$$
$$= 225 + 289$$
$$= 514$$

- Take the **square root** of the sum.
$$AB = \sqrt{514}$$
$$AB = 22.7m \ (1 \ d.p.)$$

2 Town A is 15km due north of town C. Town B is 12km due east of town A. Work out the direct distance between town B and town C.

$$(CB)^2 = 15^2 + 12^2$$
$$(CB)^2 = 225 + 144$$
$$(CB)^2 = 369$$
$$CB = \sqrt{369}$$
$$CB = 19.2km \ (3 \ s.f.)$$

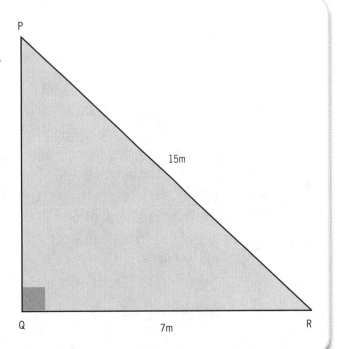

Finding the Length of a Shorter Side

The method for finding the length of the shorter side is the same as finding the hypotenuse. Remember, instead of adding the two sides together you subtract the smaller value from the larger value.

Example

Find the length of PQ in the triangle alongside. Give your answer to one decimal place.

- $$(PR)^2 = (PQ)^2 + (QR)^2$$
$$15^2 = (PQ)^2 + 7^2$$
- $$15^2 - 7^2 = (PQ)^2$$
$$225 - 49 = (PQ)^2$$
$$176 = (PQ)^2$$
- $$PQ = \sqrt{176}$$
$$PQ = 13.3m \ (1 \ d.p.)$$

Pythagoras' Theorem

Applications of Pythagoras' Theorem

Pythagoras' Theorem can be used to solve problems.

Examples

1 A ladder of 12m in length rests against a wall. The foot of the ladder is 6.8m away from the wall. How high up the wall does the ladder reach? Give your answer to 3 s.f.

Call the height of the wall h.
$$12^2 = h^2 + 6.8^2$$
$$12^2 - 6.8^2 = h^2$$
$$144 - 46.24 = h^2$$
$$h^2 = 97.76$$
$$h = \sqrt{97.76}$$
$$h = 9.89\text{m}$$

The height that the ladder reaches up the wall is 9.89m.

2 Calculate the length of a line XY, which connects X (2, 5) and Y (5, 12). Give your answer to 3 s.f.

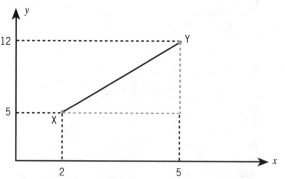

Diagram not drawn to scale

Horizontal distance = 3
Vertical distance = 7

$$\text{Length of } (XY)^2 = 3^2 + 7^2$$
$$= 9 + 49$$
$$= 58$$
$$XY = \sqrt{58}$$
$$XY = 7.62 \text{ (3 s.f.)}$$

Quick Test

1 The hypotenuse is the longest side of a right angled triangle. True or false?
2 Explain what other property a hypotenuse has.
3 Two sides of a right angled triangle are 3cm and 4cm. What is the length of the hypotenuse?
   a) 12cm **b)** 7cm **c)** 25cm **d)** 5cm
4 The length x of this triangle to 1 d.p. is 7.1cm. True or false?

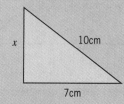

© Lonsdale

Skills Practice

1 Work out the missing length, x, in each of the triangles below.

a)
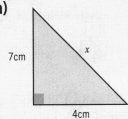
7cm
4cm
x

b)
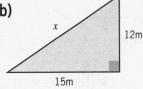
x
12m
15m

c)
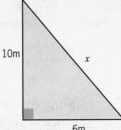
10m
6m
x

d)
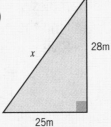
x
28m
25m

e)
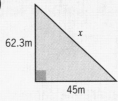
62.3m
x
45m

f)
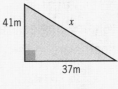
41m
x
37m

g)
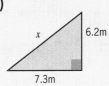
x
6.2m
7.3m

h)
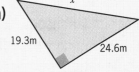
x
19.3m
24.6m

2 Work out the missing length, y, in each of the triangles below.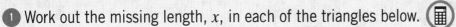

a)
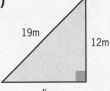
19m
12m
y

b)
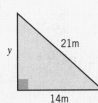
y
21m
14m

c)
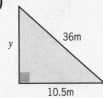
y
36m
10.5m

d)
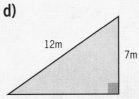
12m
7m
y

e)
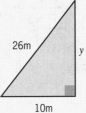
26m
y
10m

f)
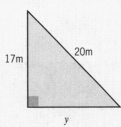
17m
20m
y

g)
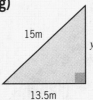
15m
y
13.5m

h)
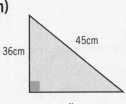
36cm
45cm
y

3 The diagram shows a rectangle of length 12cm and width 9cm.
Work out the length of the diagonal of the rectangle.

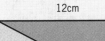
12cm
9cm

4 Work out the perimeter of the triangle below. Give your answer to one decimal place.

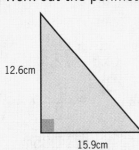
12.6cm
15.9cm

Similarity

Similar figures

Similar figures are those that are the same shape but different sizes. For example, models are similar to real-life objects.

For similar shapes, corresponding angles are equal and **corresponding** lengths are in the same **ratio**.

Corresponding sides are in the same ratio. The length of the bigger triangle is twice the size of the small triangle.

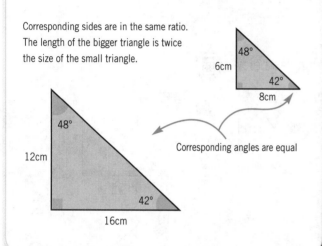

Corresponding angles are equal

Finding Missing Lengths

Use the following to work out the missing lengths of similar figures.

Examples

① Find the missing length x.
Give your answer to 3 s.f.

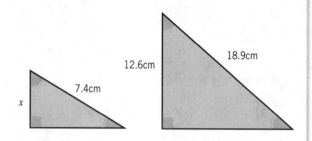

Since the corresponding sides are in the same ratio

$$\frac{x}{7.4} = \frac{12.6}{18.9}$$

Multiply both sides by 7.4

$$x = \frac{12.6}{18.9} \times 7.4$$

$$x = 4.9\dot{3}$$

② Find the missing length x.

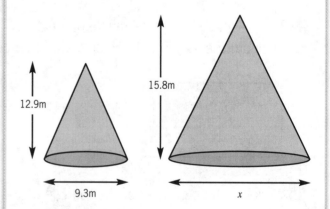

Since the corresponding sides are in the same ratio

$$\frac{x}{15.8} = \frac{9.3}{12.4}$$

Multiply both sides by 15.8

$$x = \frac{9.3}{12.4} \times 15.8$$

$$x = 11.85m$$

Skills Practice

1 Work out the missing length x in each pair of similar shapes below. Give your answer to one decimal place.

a)

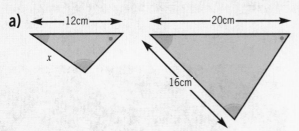

12cm
x
20cm
16cm

b)

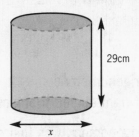

21.5cm
15cm
29cm
x

c)

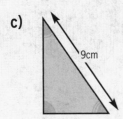 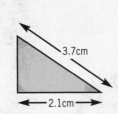

9cm
x
3.7cm
2.1cm

d)

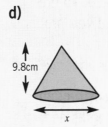 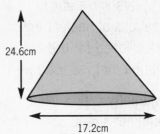

9.8cm
x
24.6cm
17.2cm

e)

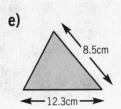 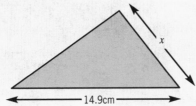

8.5cm
12.3cm
x
14.9cm

2 Decide whether each pair of shapes is similar or not similar.

a)

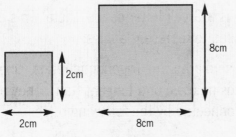

2cm
2cm
8cm
8cm

b)

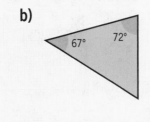

67° 72°
72°
41°

c)

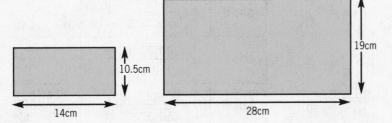

10.5cm
14cm
19cm
28cm

d)

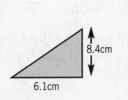 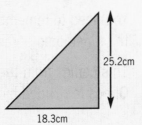

8.4cm
6.1cm
25.2cm
18.3cm

e)

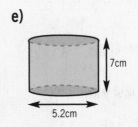 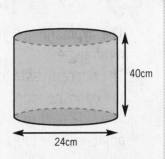

7cm
5.2cm
40cm
24cm

Trigonometry

Trigonometry

Trigonometry connects the sides and angles of right angled triangles.

Trigonometry was first developed about 4000 years ago and can be traced to the civilizations of ancient Egypt. It was probably first developed for use in sailing as a navigation method used with astronomy.

Trigonometry is now used in construction and engineering to work out lengths and angles on plans.

Labelling the Sides of the Triangle

In this triangle:

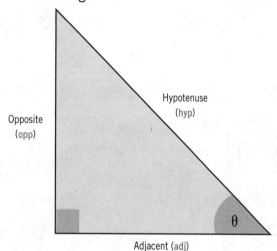

- The **hypotenuse** (hyp) is opposite the right angle.
- The opposite side to the angle θ is called the **opposite** (opp).
- The side next to the angle θ is called the **adjacent** side (adj).

θ is a Greek letter called Theta. This is often used to represent angles.

There are three trigonomic ratios, **sine** (sin), **cosine** (cos) and **tangent** (tan). They are connected by the following rules:

sin θ	$\dfrac{\text{opposite}}{\text{hypotenuse}}$	$\dfrac{\text{opp}}{\text{hyp}}$
cos θ	$\dfrac{\text{adjacent}}{\text{hypotenuse}}$	$\dfrac{\text{adj}}{\text{hyp}}$
tan θ	$\dfrac{\text{opposite}}{\text{adjacent}}$	$\dfrac{\text{opp}}{\text{adj}}$

You need to remember these. Most people use the mnemonic phrase **SOH – CAH – TOA**

This comes from the first letters of **S**in equals **O**pposite divided by **H**ypotenuse, etc.

Finding the Length of a Side

To solve a trigonometric problem there are several steps.

Example
Calculate the length of x in this triangle.

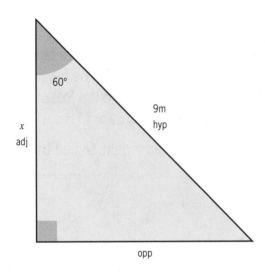

1. Label the sides of the triangle relative to the angle given.

2. Decide on the ratio. In this case use cosine ratio.

$$\cos 60° = \frac{adj}{hyp}$$

3. Substitute the values into the ratio.

$$\cos 60° = \frac{x}{9}$$

$$9 \times \cos 60° = x \quad \longleftarrow \text{ Rearrange the formula to find } x$$

$$x = 4.5m$$

Make sure that you know how to key this into your calculator.

Calculating the Size of an Angle

The method of calculating an angle is similar to finding the length of a side.

Example
Calculate the angle PQR.

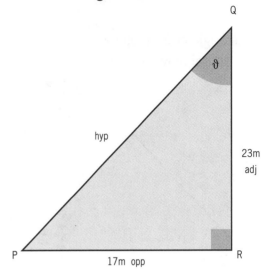

1. Label the sides of the triangle relative to the angle you're finding.

2. Decide on the ratio. In this case use the tangent ratio.

$$\tan \theta = \frac{opp}{adj}$$

$$\tan \theta = \frac{17}{23}$$

$$\tan \theta = 0.739...\text{(keep all the digits on your calculator display)}$$

$$\theta = \tan^{-1} 0.739... \quad \longleftarrow \begin{array}{l}\theta = \tan^{-1} 0.739... \text{ means the} \\ \text{inverse tan of } 0.739..., \\ \text{which is the angle that has} \\ \text{a tan of } 0.739.\end{array}$$

$$\theta = 36.5° \text{ to 1 d.p.}$$

Make sure you know how your calculator works in order to calculate these equations.

Trigonometry

Angles of Elevation and Depression

- The **angle of elevation** is measured from the horizontal upwards.

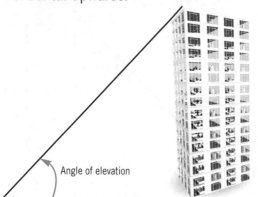

Angle of elevation

- The **angle of depression** is measured from the horizontal downwards.

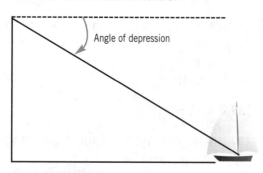

Angle of depression

Example

John looks down from a cliff to a boat below. The angle of depression is 52°. The height of the cliff is 100m. How far from the foot of the cliff is the boat? Give your answer to 3 s.f.

Put this information into a right angled triangle.

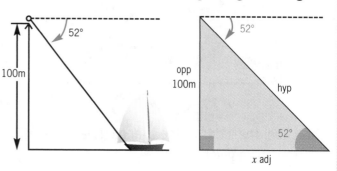

$$\tan 52° = \frac{opp}{adj}$$
$$\tan 52° = \frac{100}{x}$$
$$x \times \tan 52° = 100 \quad \leftarrow \text{Rearrange to make } x \text{ the subject}$$
$$x = \frac{100}{\tan 52°}$$
$$x = 78.1\text{m (3 s.f.)}$$

Quick Test

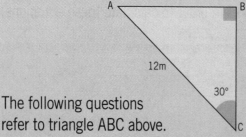

The following questions refer to triangle ABC above.

1. What is the length of AB in relation to BCA?
   a) Hypotenuse **b)** Opposite **c)** Adjacent
2. The length AC is the hypotenuse. True or false?
3. If the length AB is being calculated, which ratio would you use?
4. Work out the length of AB.

1 For each of the triangles below, work out the value of x.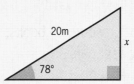

a)
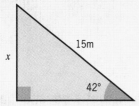
15m
x
42°

d)
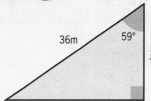
36m
59°
x

b)
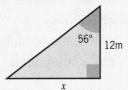
56°
12m
x

e)
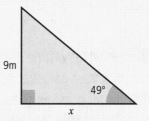
20m
x
78°

c)
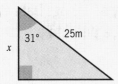
31° 25m
x

f)
9m
49°
x

2 For each of the triangles below, work out the size of angle x.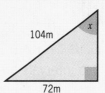

a)
x
15m
9m

d)

104m
x
72m

b)
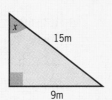
15m
x
12m

e)
x
9cm
6cm

c)
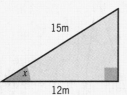
24m
x
31m

f)
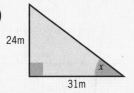
12cm
x
20cm

3 Mehnaz stands 25m from the base of a 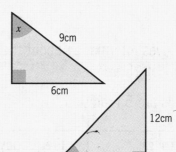 tower. She measures the angle of elevation from ground level to the top of the tower as 55°. Calculate the height of the tower. Give your answer to 3 s.f.

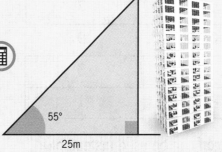
55°
25m

4 For the rectangle opposite work out the angle between the 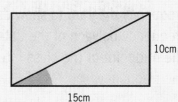 diagonal and the base. Give your answer to 3 s.f.

10cm
15cm

Handling Data

Collecting Data

Remember that there are several ways to collect data:
- Information from resources: books, the Internet and newspapers.
- Data collection sheets.
- Experiments.
- Questionnaires.

Keep the questions simple when writing questionnaires. Ensure that your personal opinion doesn't show and allow for all possible outcomes.

Make sure when carrying out a questionnaire that you don't introduce bias. For example, if you're conducting a questionnaire on coffee consumption you wouldn't stand outside a cafe and ask people which coffee they prefer.

Continuous data is found by measuring whilst discrete data is found by counting. Data that has been collected can be put into a frequency table.

Representing Data

One way to represent continuous data is to put it into class intervals; the class intervals are usually equal in width.

Example
The table below gives information about the weights, in grams, of 25 apples.

The class intervals are 5 grams.

Weight (w g)	Frequency
$90 \leqslant w < 95$	5
$95 \leqslant w < 100$	7
$100 \leqslant w < 105$	9
$105 \leqslant w < 110$	3
$110 \leqslant w < 115$	1

A frequency polygon can be used instead of a frequency diagram to show data. To draw a frequency polygon of the data above, plot the midpoint of the class interval against the frequency.

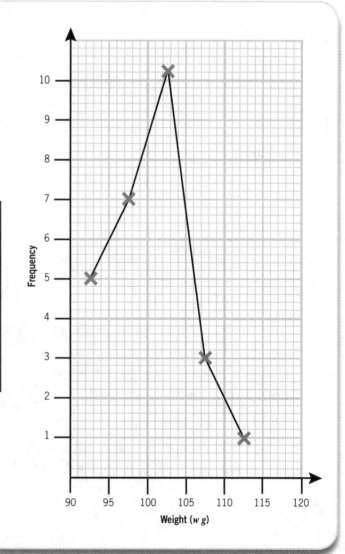

Pie Charts

Remember each section in a **pie chart** represents a certain number of items.

Example

Will counted 24 cars in a car park and noted their colour. The table shows his results.

Car colour	Blue	Red	Silver	Black
Frequency	4	5	9	6

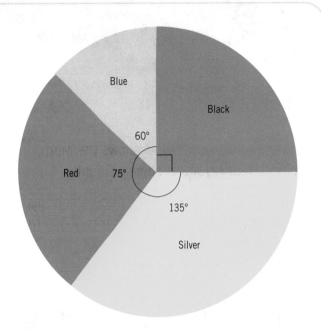

Draw a pie chart.
- Draw a circle and mark the centre.
- Work out the angles.

$$\frac{360}{24} = 15°$$

1 car represents 15°.
Multiply each colour by 15.

Blue: 4 × 15 = 60°
Red: 5 × 15 = 75°
Silver: 9 × 15 = 135°
Black: 6 × 15 = 90°

Scatterdiagrams and Correlation

As a quick reminder there are three types of **correlation**:

1. **Positive correlation** – both values increase.
2. **Negative correlation** – one value increases and the other decreases.
3. **Zero correlation** – no linear correlation between variables.

Handling Data

Lines of Best Fit

The **scatterdiagram** below shows the Maths and Science test results of some students.

A line of best fit has been added, which has roughly the same number of points above the line as below it.

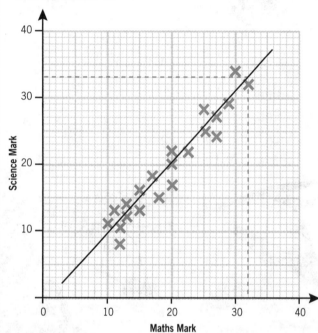

There is a positive correlation. The higher the student's Maths score the higher their Science score.

For example, a score of 32 on the Maths test is approximately a score of 33 on the Science test.

Scatterdiagrams can easily be drawn using a spreadsheet package on a computer.

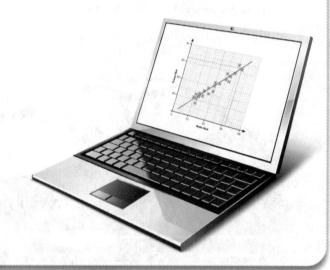

Quick Test

1. For $20 \leqslant h < 30$, the class interval is 10. True or false?
2. For this scatter diagram, what type of correlation is shown?

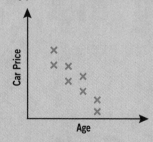

3. A frequency polygon joins the midpoints of the class intervals. True or false?

Skills Practice

1 Erin carried out a survey on how often people use a leisure centre. She did her survey by standing outside the leisure centre on a Tuesday morning. Explain why her results may be biased.

2 Draw a frequency polygon of this data on the graph paper below.

Height (*h* cm)	Frequency
$0 \leq h < 20$	3
$20 \leq h < 40$	5
$40 \leq h < 60$	6
$60 \leq h < 80$	10
$80 \leq h < 100$	9
$100 \leq h < 120$	4
$120 \leq h < 140$	1

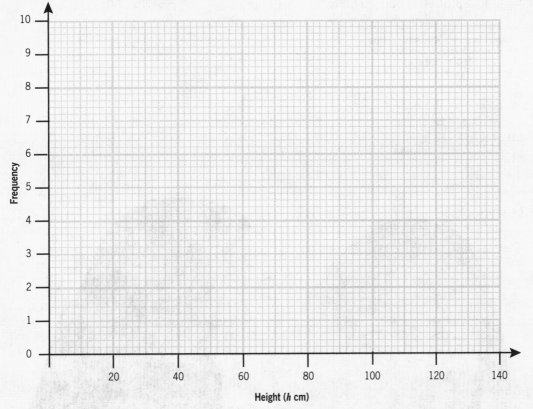

3 Draw a pie chart of this data:

Travel to school	Walk	Car	Bus	Bike
Frequency	16	4	20	5

Averages

Averages from a Frequency Table

The average you calculate from a frequency table will not always be a whole number.

Example

The **frequency** table shows the number of sisters 12 students had:

Number of Sisters (x)	Frequency
0	5
1	3
2	2
3	2

The table shows that 5 students had no sisters.

$$\text{Mean} = \frac{\text{Total of frequency} \times \text{Number of sisters}}{\text{Total of frequency}}$$

$$\text{Mean} = \frac{(0 \times 5) + (1 \times 3) + (2 \times 2) + (3 \times 2)}{5 + 3 + 2 + 2}$$

$$\text{Mean} = \frac{0 + 3 + 4 + 6}{12}$$

$$= \frac{13}{12}$$

$$= 1.08\overset{..}{3} \text{ sisters.}$$

Median

Since there are 12 students the **median** must lie between the 6th and 7th students.

Counting up the frequency column gives the 6th and 7th students having three sisters.

Mode

The number of sisters that occurs the most is none. So the **mode** of the data is none.

Range

The **range** of sisters is...

$$\text{Range} = \text{Highest number} - \text{Lowest number}$$
$$\text{of sisters} \qquad \text{of sisters}$$
$$3 - 0$$

$$= 3 \text{ sisters}$$

Averages of Grouped Data

Continuous data is grouped into class intervals since the exact data set is not known.

The mean can be estimated by using the midpoint of the class interval. The midpoint is the halfway value.

Weight (w kg)	Frequency (f)	Midpoint (x)	fx
40 ≤ w < 45	6	42.5	255
45 ≤ w < 50	5	47.5	237.5
50 ≤ w < 55	3	52.5	157.5
55 ≤ w < 60	2	57.5	115
60 ≤ w < 65	1	62.5	62.5
Total	17		827.5

Adding these extra columns helps to show working out

Example

The table opposite shows the weight (w kg) of some year 10 students.

$\sum f$ means 'the sum of f'.

$$\text{mean} = \frac{\sum fx}{\sum f}$$
$$= \frac{827.5}{17}$$

mean = 48.7kg (1 d.p.)

Modal class is 40 ≤ w < 45

The class interval containing the median is:
45 ≤ w < 50
Since there are 17 students, the median must be in the class interval in which the 9th student lies.

Quick Test

1. Find the mean of the data below.

a)

Number of Brothers (x)	Frequency
0	4
1	5
2	3
3	2

b) The mode of the data is 5.
   True or false?

c) The median of the data is 1.
   True or false?

d) The range of the data is 0 – 3.
   True or false?

KEY WORDS

Make sure you understand these words before moving on!
- Frequency
- Mean
- Median
- Mode
- Range
- Continuous data
- Class interval
- Modal class

Averages

Skills Practice

1. Molly made this table to show how many minutes (t) late students were for registration.

Number of Minutes Late (t)	0	1	2	3	4	5	6
Frequency (f)	14	2	2	1	3	1	1

Calculate...

a) the mean   **b)** the median   **c)** the mode   **d)** the range

2. The table shows the height (h cm) of some year 7 students.

Height (h cm)	Frequency (f)
$130 \leq h < 135$	5
$135 \leq h < 140$	7
$140 \leq h < 145$	4
$145 \leq h < 150$	3
$150 \leq h < 155$	2

a) Calculate an estimate for the mean height of this data.

b) Write down the modal class.

c) Which class interval has the median height?

3 The table shows the weight (*w* kg) of some year 7 students.

Weight (*w* kg)	Frequency (*f*)
$30 \leqslant w < 40$	4
$40 \leqslant w < 50$	8
$50 \leqslant w < 60$	12
$60 \leqslant w < 70$	3
$70 \leqslant w < 80$	3

a) Calculate an estimate for the mean weight of this data.

b) Write down the modal class.

c) Which class interval has the median weight?

4 The table shows information about the number of minutes some students spent doing homework on one evening.

Number of Minutes (*t*)	Frequency (*f*)
$0 < t \leqslant 20$	10
$20 < t \leqslant 40$	15
$40 < t \leqslant 60$	25
$60 < t \leqslant 80$	8
$80 < t \leqslant 100$	2

a) Find the class interval that contains the median.

b) Work out an estimate for the mean number of minutes that the students spent doing homework.

Cumulative Frequency Graphs

Cumulative Frequency Graphs

Cumulative frequency graphs are very useful for finding the median and spread of grouped data.

Example
The table shows information about the amount of time 50 students spent doing homework one evening.

Time (x minutes)	Frequency
$0 < x \leqslant 10$	5
$10 < x \leqslant 20$	12
$20 < x \leqslant 30$	17
$30 < x \leqslant 40$	10
$40 < x \leqslant 50$	4
$50 < x \leqslant 60$	2

A cumulative frequency table can be drawn for this data.

When a cumulative frequency graph is drawn, plot the upper class boundaries, so plot (10, 5) (20, 17) (30, 34) (40, 44) (50, 48) (60, 50). Join the points with a smooth curve.

Time (x minutes)	Cumulative Frequency
$0 < x \leqslant 10$	5
$0 < x \leqslant 20$	(5 + 12 =) 17
$0 < x \leqslant 30$	(17 + 17 =) 34
$0 < x \leqslant 40$	(34 + 10 =) 44
$0 < x \leqslant 50$	(44 + 4 =) 48
$0 < x \leqslant 60$	(48 + 2 =) 50

To complete the cumulative frequency column add the frequencies.

Cumulative frequency graphs are S-shaped.

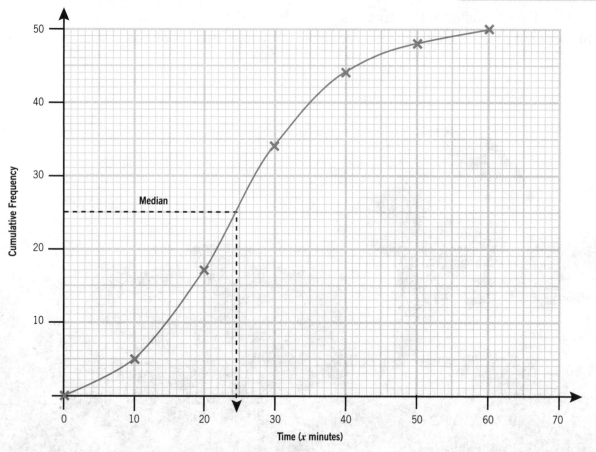

Cumulative Frequency Graphs (cont.)

The median is the middle value of the distribution.

Median = $\frac{1}{2}$ × total of cumulative frequency

$= \frac{1}{2} \times 50 = 25$

Reading across on the previous page from 25 to the y axis and then down gives a median time of approximately 24.5 minutes.

Finding the Interquartile Range

The **upper quartile** is the value three quarters of the way into the distribution.

$\frac{3}{4} \times 50 = 37.5$

Using the graph below gives an approximate time of 32.5 minutes.

The **lower quartile** is the value one quarter of the way into the distribution.

$\frac{1}{4} \times 50 = 12.5$

Using the graph gives an approximate time of 16.5 minutes.

The **interquartile range** is found by subtracting the lower quartile from the upper quartile.

Interquartile range	=	upper quartile	–	lower quartile

The interquartile range would be:

Interquartile range = upper quartile – lower quartile

$= 32.5 - 16.5$

$= 16$ minutes.

A large interquartile range indicates that the middle half of the data is widely spread about the median.

A small interquartile range indicates that the middle half of the data is concentrated about the median.

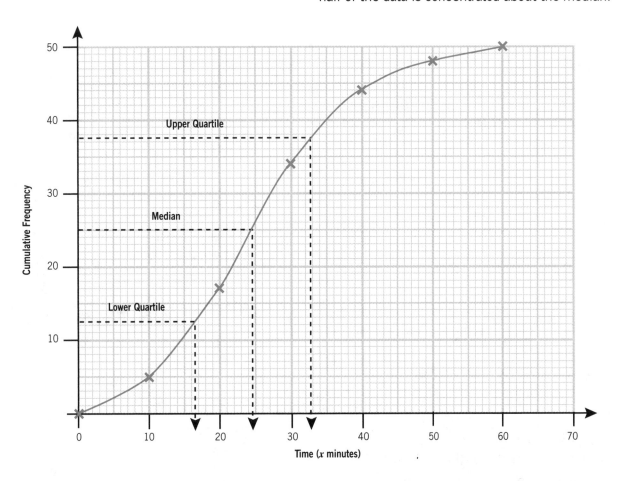

Cumulative Frequency Graphs

Box Plots

A box plot shows the interquartile range as a box, which makes it useful when comparing distributions.

The box plot for the homework data on p.78 would look like this:

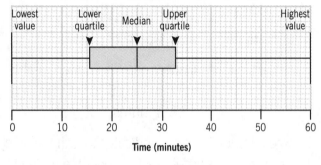

Example

The times in seconds taken by 11 students to solve a puzzle is listed in order:

3, 3, 5, 6, 7, 7, 8, 9, 11, 13, 14

Draw a plot of this data.

3, 3, ⑤, 6, 7, ⑦, 8, 9, ⑪, 13, 14

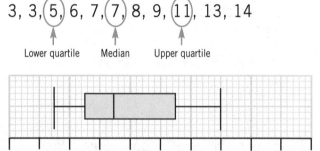

Quick Test

1. These two box plots show the results of two classes, R and T, who took the same maths test.

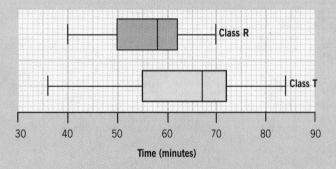

   a) Which class has the student who scored the lowest mark?

   b) What was the median mark of class T?

   c) The students in class R generally did better in the test than those students in class T. True or false?

   d) The interquartile range of marks was larger in class R than class T. True or false?

KEY WORDS

Make sure you understand these words before moving on!

* Cumulative frequency graphs
* Median
* Upper quartile
* Lower quartile
* Interquartile range

1 The following data shows the distance (*d* km) from a shopping centre.

Distance (*d* km)	Frequency	Cumulative Frequency
$0 \leqslant d < 5$	8	
$5 \leqslant d < 10$	22	
$10 \leqslant d < 15$	25	
$15 \leqslant d < 20$	18	
$20 \leqslant d < 25$	14	
$25 \leqslant d < 30$	3	

a) Complete the cumulative frequency column in the table above.

b) On the graph paper below, complete the cumulative frequency graph.

c) Use your graph to find the median distance.

d) Use your graph to find the interquartile range.

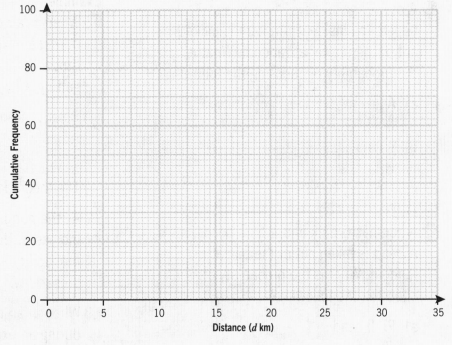

e) On the graph paper opposite, draw a box plot of the data.

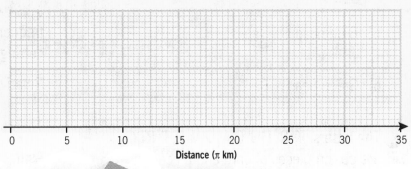

Probability

Theoretical Probability

The theoretical **probability** can be calculated in the following way:

Probability of an outcome or P (outcome)	=	Number of ways an outcome can happen / Total number of outcomes

Examples

1 A drawer has 3 keys, 4 coins and 2 paperclips inside it. An item is picked out of the drawer at random. What is the probability of choosing the following?

a) A key
$$\frac{3}{9} = \frac{1}{3}$$

b) A coin
$$\frac{4}{9}$$

c) A rubber band
$$0$$

2 A bag has 6 pink and 4 blue beads. A bead is taken out of the bag at random. What is the probability of choosing the following?

a) Pink bead
$$\frac{6}{10} = \frac{3}{5}$$

b) Blue bead
$$\frac{4}{10} = \frac{2}{5}$$

c) Green bead
$$0$$

3 The letters T R I G O N O M E T R Y are put on pieces of card and placed in a bag. A piece of card is chosen at random. What is the probability of choosing the following?
a) The letter M = $\frac{1}{12}$
b) The letter T = $\frac{2}{12} = \frac{1}{6}$
c) A vowel = $\frac{4}{12} = \frac{1}{3}$
d) The letter K = 0

Experimental Probability

The experimental probability (**relative frequency**) can be calculated in the following way:

Experimental probability	=	Number of times the outcome happened / Total number of times experiment carried out

Examples

1 When a fair dice was thrown 120 times during an experiment, a five came up 16 times. What is the relative frequency of getting a five?

$$\text{Relative frequency} = \frac{16}{120}$$
$$= \frac{2}{15}$$

The theoretical probability of a five $= \frac{1}{6}$

As the number of times a dice is thrown increases, the nearer the experimental probability approaches the theoretical probability.

2 When a fair coin was thrown 250 times during an experiment, a tail came up 138 times. What is the relative frequency and theoretical probability of getting a tail?

$$\text{Relative frequency} = \frac{138}{250}$$

Theoretical probability of a tail $= \frac{1}{2}$

As the number of times the coin is thrown increases, the experimental probability approaches the theoretical probability.

The Language of Probability

The language of probability is often seen in newspapers.

Olympic Bid

It seemed **unlikely** in the run up to the decision about the 2012 Olympic Games that London would win. The **probability** that Paris would be chosen was always very high. It was just that the other contenders had **little chance** of success when the final presentations were given.

Probability of an Event Not Happening

Mutually exclusive events are events that can't happen at the same time.

If two outcomes of an event are mutually exclusive, then:

P (outcome will happen) = 1 − P (outcome won't happen)

or

P (outcome will not happen) = 1 − P (outcome will happen)

Example

The probability that Sasoon is late is 0.31. What is the probability that he isn't late?

$$P \text{ (not late)} = 1 - P \text{ (late)}$$
$$= 1 - 0.31$$
$$= 0.69$$

The probability that it rains on a particular day in August is $\frac{3}{11}$. What is the probability that it does not rain in August?

$$P \text{ (not rain)} = 1 - P \text{ (rains)}$$
$$= 1 - \frac{3}{11}$$
$$= \frac{8}{11}$$

Probability

Possible Outcomes for Two or More Events

A **sample space diagram** can be helpful when considering the outcomes of two or more events.

Example

Two fair dice are thrown at the same time and their scores are added together. Draw a diagram to show all the possible outcomes.

1 P (score of 4)

$$= \frac{3}{36} = \frac{1}{12}$$

2 P (score of 9)

$$= \frac{4}{36} = \frac{1}{9}$$

First Dice

†	1	2	3	4	5	6
1	2	3	④	5	6	7
2	3	④	5	6	7	8
3	④	5	6	7	8	9
4	5	6	7	8	9	10
5	6	7	8	9	10	11
6	7	8	9	10	11	12

Second Dice

The Addition Law

In the **addition law**, if two or more events are mutually exclusive, the probability of A or B or C, etc. is found by adding the probabilities.

> P (A or B or C...) = P (A) + P (B) + P (C) + ...

The Multiplication Law

The **multiplication law** is used when two events are independent whilst the outcome of the second event is not affected by the outcome of the first event.

The probability of A and B and C happening together is:

> P (A and B and C) = P (A) × P (B) × P (C)

Tree Diagrams

Tree diagrams are another way of showing the possible **outcomes** of two or more **events**.

Example

A bag has 3 red and 4 blue buttons in it. A button is taken from the bag at random and its colour noted. The button is then replaced. A second button is taken from the bag and its colour noted.

Draw a tree diagram of the information.

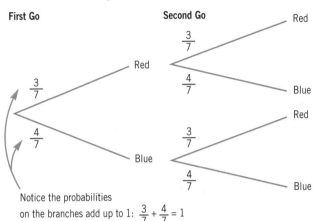

First Go   **Second Go**

Notice the probabilities on the branches add up to 1: $\frac{3}{7} + \frac{4}{7} = 1$

a) Find the probability of picking two red buttons:

$$P \text{ (Red and Red)} = P \text{ (Red)} \times P \text{ (Red)}$$
$$= \frac{3}{7} \times \frac{3}{7}$$
$$= \frac{9}{49}$$

> The multiplication law P (A and B) = P (A) × P (B)

b) Find the probability of picking one of either colour:

$$P \text{ (Red and Blue)} = P \text{ (Red)} \times P \text{ (Blue)}$$
$$= \frac{3}{7} \times \frac{4}{7}$$
$$= \frac{12}{49}$$

or $P \text{ (Blue and Red)} = P \text{ (Blue)} \times P \text{ (Red)}$
$$= \frac{4}{7} \times \frac{3}{7}$$
$$= \frac{12}{49}$$

> The multiplication law P (A or B) = P (A) + P (B)

c) $P \text{ (one of each colour)} = \frac{12}{49} + \frac{12}{49}$
$$= \frac{24}{49}$$

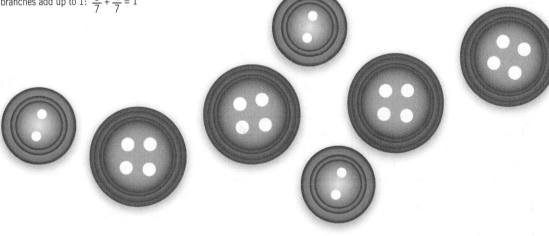

Quick Test

1. What is the probability of getting a 7 on a fair dice? **a)** 1 **b)** $\frac{1}{2}$ **c)** 0 **d)** $\frac{1}{6}$
2. The probability that it will rain is $\frac{4}{9}$. What is the probability that it will not rain?
3. If a fair coin is thrown 500 times, approximately how many heads would you expect?
4. P (A or B) = P (A) × P (B). True or false?

Probability

1. A bag has 6 red, 3 blue and 2 yellow beads. A bead is taken out of the bag at random. What is the probability of choosing the following:
   a) A red bead.
   b) A yellow bead.
   c) Not a blue bead.
   d) A red or blue bead.

2. The probability that the Bank of England base rate will go below 0.5% is 0.15. Work out the probability that the base rate will not go below 0.5%.

3. The probability that Ryan is late for school is 0.42. Work out the probability that Ryan is not late for school.

4. Rupert roles a fair 6-sided dice once. Write down the probability that the dice will show a 3 or a 4.

5. A fair dice is thrown 300 times. How many fives would you expect to appear?

6. Amy plays a game of chess. She can win or draw or lose the game.

   a) The table shows the probabilities that she will win or draw the game.

Result	Win	Draw	Lose
Probability	0.4	0.3	

   Work out the probability that she will lose the game.

   b) If Amy plays 50 games of chess, how many would you expect her to win?

7 The tree diagram shows the outcomes of throwing two coins.

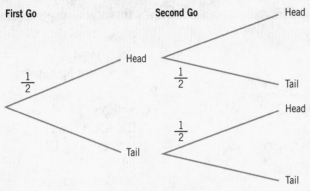

First Go   Second Go   Head

Head

$\frac{1}{2}$ $\frac{1}{2}$ Tail

Head

$\frac{1}{2}$

Tail

Tail

a) Complete the tree diagram.

b) Work out the probability of getting two heads.

c) Work out the probability of a head and a tail in any order.

8 A bag has 4 red and 5 green beads. A bead is chosen from the bag at random, its colour noted and then it is replaced. A second bead is then taken. The tree diagram shows the results.

First Go   Second Go   Red

$\frac{4}{9}$

Red

$\frac{4}{9}$ $\frac{5}{9}$ Green

Red

$\frac{5}{9}$ $\frac{4}{9}$

Green

$\frac{5}{9}$ Green

a) Work out the probability of getting two green beads.

b) Work out the probability of getting a bead of either colour.

Index